MASTER THE KEY

A STORY TO FREE YOUR POTENTIAL, FIND

MEANING AND LIVE LIFE ON PURPOSE

MIKE FLYNN

Master The Key

First Edition

eBook: 978-1-5445-0206-9
Paperback: 978-1-5445-0207-6
Hardcover: 978-1-5445-0208-3

Printed in the United States of America

TABLE OF CONTENTS

Foreword ix

Introduction... xiii

THE CALL

Shattered.. 19

Waking Up.. 29

The Recovery..35

STORY

The Janitor 43

Angelica.. 49

The Choice 57

The Wine Cellar 65

The Greatest Treasure.....................................73

Reflect and Respond....................................... 83

GIFTS

Meeting Chaz 91

The Audition 97

Rediscover Gifts...105

The Affirmation...115

Reflect and Respond.......................................121

ACTION

Meeting Fidel.. 127

Setting Sail 137

Shifting Gears.. 145

Reflect and Respond.. 153

COMMUNITY

Lucy meets The Janitor..159

Meeting Bill 163

The Stuff 171

The Surprise 179

Reflect and Respond.. 183

Giving Thanks... 189

About Mike 193

Kind Words

"We all experience adversity and how we respond to it is up to us. Life is a matter of choices. This book teaches timeless lessons on the power of choosing to own your story, gifts, action, and community. A must read for anyone seeking personal growth."

- **Lou Holtz**, *College Football Hall of Fame Coach, speaker, New York Times best-selling author, and analyst*

"Sometimes life throws you a gut punch and it can be hard to know where to go from there. This inspiring story reminds us how important it is to stay open to opportunities that may lead you to places you never imagined."

- **Mel Robbins**, *Author of the international best-seller, The 5 Second Rule*

"Mike reminds us that no matter who we are, where we are or what role we are playing, we each have the opportunity to direct the narrative of our life story and create a path towards a positive future!

- **Jon Gordon**, *Best-Selling author of The Carpenter and The Seed*

"True leaders clear a path for a better future and Mike artfully shares with readers exactly how to do so. He brilliantly simplifies the complexities of choosing our own story and defining our own worth by handing us the Master key to unlock our best self. Thank you, Mike, for all the brilliant questions, and for a very good reason to enter our own caves and sip some fine wine."

- **AmyK Hutchens**, *Award Winning International Speaker, Author and Business*
Strategist

"Master the Key is a profoundly poignant story that is sure to have a positive impact on your life – and maybe even save it. I highly recommend this book."

- **Jim Afremow**, *author of The Champion's Mind*

"We've all made the mistake of grinding away in order to achieve something someone else said would fulfill us. And when it doesn't, our light begins to dim. Master The Key reminds us that we each possess the key to setting our potential free without losing who we are in the process."

- **Sheryl O'Loughlin**, *CEO of REBBL Inc, former CEO of Clif Bar and former Executive Director, Center For Entrepreneurial Studies at Stanford Graduate School of Business*

"God has given us everything we need to achieve His purposes for our life. Mike's new book is a beautiful illustration of how to set your unlimited potential, completely free."

- **Greg Amundson**, *former DEA Special Agent, #1 bestselling author of The Warrior and The Monk, and plank-owner of the Eagle Rise Speakers Bureau*

"There's no question that finding and starting with why is important. And still, Mike's powerful story-telling reminds us that before we can do either, we must remember we are worthy of a why in the first place. A must read for any organization in the people business."

- Kara Goldin, *Founder and CEO of hint, Inc*

Believing our thoughts is a sacred practice. If we believe false stories and made-up scenarios, we will limit our ultimate potential. Master the Key gives us the space to understand those limits to our potential and change the story indefinitely.

- **Caroline Burckle**, 2008 *Olympic Bronze Medalist and Co-Founder of RISE Athletes*

There are many people to be thanked but only a few to whom this book is dedicated:

To my wife, Lisa: you are my biggest fan and cheerleader. Thank you for being in my corner, even in the most uncertain of times. You have always believed in me and my potential. I am forever grateful to you.

"To Us."

To my children: I believe in each of you. God has created you with so many gifts and talents. You each have a wonderful sense of curiosity and a strong desire to learn. Those two characteristics will take you very far in life. Remember, life's challenges can and will work for your good if you allow them to.

෨෬

FOREWORD

One of my favorite activities is cycling. Whether it's road biking or mountain biking, I love how the sport mimics some parts of life. There are times when you can simply cruise and enjoy all that is around you. Occasions that require your complete and total focus while you safely fly downhill at breakneck speeds. And still, other moments when one must put their head down, foot to the pedal and climb.

I enjoy the cruising and soaring more than the climbing, but the climb is the most rewarding and gives me the greatest sense of fulfillment. It's just me, the road and my thoughts. One of the things I reflect on most, especially during difficult climbs, is all the people who have prepared me for life's most challenging ascents. My mother, my wife, my children, my dear friend, Stephen Covey, and many others who have all joined me at various times in the pursuit to set my potential free, find meaning and live life on purpose.

In my book, *Aspire: Discovering Your Purpose Through The Power of Words*, I share a story about a chance encounter I had with Dr. Gerald Bell, one of Michael Jordan's mindset coaches and the founder of The Bell Leadership Institute. I was preparing to lead a troop of scouts on a grueling twenty-mile hike and before we got underway I shared the story of how Dr. Bell prepared Michael Jordan, then a freshman at the University of North Carolina, and his teammates to pursue a National Championship before the season even started. Dr. Bell and Head Coach, Dean Smith, hung posters of the Louisiana Superdome on every locker. It served as a reminder of what they could achieve if they gave their all, not just to the season, but in everything. It also served as a reminder that they were worthy of it.

Let me pause here a moment and ask you a question: what poster is hanging in your locker? Does it lift you up? Does it remind you of what you're capable of? Is it something you want to move toward or away from?

The way Mike and I met involves a dash of serendipity. Like many Americans, Mike had been crushed by the financial crisis. His finances dwindled, his health and overall sense of worth plummeted while his responsibilities to those around him increased. He was burned out.

Fortunately, years earlier, Mike had formed a mastermind group with eight thoughtful, intentional people one of whom was a guy named Jesse. I had recently spoken to Jesse and several of his colleagues in Seattle. Jesse bought copies of my book to handout at a mastermind meeting he was going to host. Mike was set to tell Jesse and the other members of his mastermind that he was moving on. He was done with the industry and needed a change, but he never did. Among other things, Jesse gave Mike a copy of my book. Mike realized that the words that made up the narrative he was telling himself held tremendous power. He also began to learn that he could choose to master those words and make them serve him. Up to this point, Mike and I had only met via the book.

Not long after, Mike discovered that we shared another mutual friend in a legendary human being named Philip who ultimately put the two of us in touch. The more I reflect on how we met, the more I realize that serendipity had little to do with it. After all, when we get on a path and on purpose we will meet people who have been waiting on our path all along. They were just waiting for us to get on path. I am so grateful our paths merged for Mike is definitely on path and on purpose.

Would we all like to avoid the crashes, the burnouts, the missteps and errors in judgement? Sure! But they are part of life; they are part of the sometimes painful, always beautiful, ever evolving act of becoming. It's how we respond to them that shapes how we engage in the world via our story, gifts, action and community. As the great Viktor Frankl once said, *"Everything can be taken from a man but one thing: the last of the human freedoms—to choose one's attitude in any given set of circumstances, to choose one's own way."*

Mike has written a story we can all relate to because, in some way, it is all of our story. There is a little bit of all of us weaved into each of the characters. But as the main character soon realizes, and his mentors are quick to remind him of, personal transformation is exactly that—personal. You have to be willing to engage in the process without letting a desired outcome distract you? Why? Because you might miss opportunities that present themselves along the way. Fortunately for us, Mike has given us the tools to inspire our reflection and guide how we might respond.

Namasté,

Kevin Hall

INTRODUCTION

Regardless of one's faith, most of us have heard the story of David and Goliath. The story is used to teach life lessons as much as it is to teach Christian principles. But there is this iconic moment in the story just before David, the young shepherd boy, faces the giant. David walks into King Saul's tent and volunteers to fight Goliath because everyone else—including Saul—was hiding.

The king asks David some questions, thinks about it for a moment and then ultimately says, "Yes, you can fight the giant, but you must wear my armor." David puts it on, walks around in it and then takes it off because he recognizes that wearing someone else's armor would limit, if not prevent, him from successfully executing his goal of defeating Goliath.

I invite you to also imagine this: David is in the king's tent. He has just been authorized to face Goliath on behalf of the Israelite army. The king himself offers his own armor to David; in fact, he places the armor on him. There can be no doubt that, in addition to the best armor, the king had all the best tools and weapons of war at his disposal—swords, maces, bows and arrows—you name it; the king had it. And still, David walked out with nothing but his slingshot and the confidence that he knew how to effectively use it. By the time he stepped onto the battlefield and picked up five smooth stones—stones that may have existed since the dawn of time—David had mastered the key needed to fulfill his God-given potential.

He knew things had not just happened *to* him but also *for* him.

He knew his gifts could and should be used not in the pursuit of gaining status or recognition, but instead in the pursuit of truth, beauty and goodness.

He knew what was at stake and why it mattered; so he took action. Did it involve risk? Yes! He could have died, but the alternative was unacceptable.

Ultimately, mastering his story, his gifts and his action equipped him to build a community that was curious about his success, sought out ways to collaborate and corrected him when he veered off course.

I know what you're thinking—isn't David the guy who had an affair, murdered his lover's husband and eventually lost his kingdom? The answer is yes! It begs the question *why*? Well, I believe it is because he stopped mastering the key that he had been given; it grew weak and fragile and eventually shattered. He, knowingly or unknowingly, adopted a lie that mastery is an outcome that one can arrive at. The reality is that mastery, and therefore mastering the key, is a daily, intentional pursuit. Needless to say, we all share a lot in common with David. *Master The Key: A Story To Free Your Potential* is about me; it's about you, it's about your neighbor, your friend and your family members. It's about all of us.

Each of us comes into this world in possession of the key needed to live out the fullness of our God-given potential. And just as each person is an unrepeatable miracle, as my friend Kevin would say, each key is unique and unrepeatable. It is complete and functional as much as it is vulnerable. So what happens then? Well, unlike the young David, we end up wearing other people's armor—armors not created for us. We pick up tools or weapons that we are not designed to wield. Why? Because an influential person said you've got no chance at defeating that giant using only a slingshot—a lie. We allow people, places, things, events, outcomes to take possession of our unique, unrepeatable key. Sometimes these people are well-intentioned, while at other times they are actively seeking to undermine our potential. In both cases, the key is shattered into four pieces—story, gifts, action and community. These pieces are buried within us and ours to rediscover.

As you read, you will discover the book is also separated into four parts—story, gifts, action and community. You will be taken on a journey along with Steve, the main character, to recover and rebuild your key—piece by piece. At the end of each part, you will be presented with the opportunity to reflect on your own thoughts and experiences, as well as respond and rediscover how to master the key. I've included questions or prompts to stimulate your thinking but feel free to adapt them as you see fit.

I am honored to be on this journey with you, and I am confident the best is now and the best is yet to come.

Let us begin.

Part 1
THE CALL

Shattered

To say Steve was the envy of nearly every advisor at Outlier Capital would be an understatement. He appeared to have everything. He was fit, his wife was gorgeous and his children, beautiful. He could instantly become friends with anyone and the list goes on. He may have been young, but by all accounts, he was the most successful advisor at Outlier Capital Management. And, much to the chagrin of his colleagues, he hadn't even been in the business for too long.

Two years earlier, Steve was working at a public relations firm in the city. He might have been extraordinarily successful there, but he felt the call to do something more than help people decide which brand of ice cream to buy. He wanted to be someplace where he could have a tangible impact on the the lives of others.

Suffice it to say many at Outlier wished that he had stayed where he was. It wasn't that he was a bad guy. It was quite the opposite. He was too nice. He showed appreciation toward everyone and sought to leave everyone whom he encountered better off than before. He had this drive—this mission—that people latched onto. But to his colleagues, it was just annoying.

Whats more, it was 2004 and business came easy for practically everyone, especially for Steve.

Fortunately for everyone at Outlier, Steve was still human. He worked hard and he learned to play harder. Over the years, his mission became less about impact and more about making easy money. He had descended from the stratosphere and rejoined the general population of hustlers focused on doing the minimum needed to close the next deal while reaping the greatest reward. But the good times didn't last very long.

The Great Recession had kicked everyone in the stomach. By January of 2009, everyone was feeling beat down. It wasn't a fun place to be. The easy money had dried up. More than half the firm had quit or been fired. Those who remained were focused on self-preservation. It had taken its toll on everyone, including Steve.

He had blown up to 250 pounds, his marriage was on the rocks, he rarely spent any time with his kids and he hadn't closed any new business in more than a year. It was as if life had him by the ropes and was pummeling him with body shot after body shot.

Steve was ready to throw in the towel.

He left the office at 6 p.m., which was early for him, and headed home to have dinner. When he walked in, his wife, Lucy, and his daughters, Tina and Elle, looked up with surprise. It had been months since he had joined them for dinner. They sat there stunned. No one got up to make him a plate or even make room at the table, so Steve took care of himself and squeezed in between his two girls. Everyone started eating again in an awkward silence.

"How was work, Daddy?" asked Tina, his five-year-old daughter.

"Well," said Steve, "I pretty much spent the day like every other day, preventing people from jumping off a cliff."

"Jumping off a cliff," giggled Tina. "That sounds scary."

The truth of her response caught Steve off guard, and he began to laugh hysterically. Poor Tina didn't realize what was going on and thought her dad was laughing at her and began to cry. Soon after, Elle joined in. Oddly enough, this only made Steve more hysterical. Finally, Lucy had had enough.

Slamming her hands on the table, she yelled, "Stop!"

"I can't even remember the last time you were home for dinner," she continued, "and this is what you do?"

Steve just sat quietly, stared down at his plate and shuffled his food side to side.

"Why on earth did you come home?"

"Honestly," said Steve as he pushed his chair away from the table, "it's a good question."

He got up, kissed Tina and Elle goodbye, grabbed his keys and walked out.

Steve and his family lived twenty minutes outside the city so he was glad to hit the highway, turn on some music and blow off some steam. He turned on the radio and a familiar song came pumping through the speakers. It was the chorus to *We are The Champions* by *Queen.*

Steve felt like anything but a champion. He felt like a jack of all trades and a master of none, and he didn't really feel dedicated to anything. And worse, he couldn't do anything about it. Steve felt trapped. He turned the radio off and stepped on the gas to hear the roar of his engine.

He was lost in thought when he heard an electronic beep and realized he was pulling into the Outlier building's parking garage.

"I guess I'll go back to work," Steve said. "I've got nothing better to do. Besides, I can have some bourbon and relax."

Steve made his way to Outlier's office on the fortieth floor. As he got off the elevator, he gave a nod to The Janitor who was vacuuming the lobby.

At least I don't have it as bad as that guy, Steve thought to himself as he made his way to his prized corner office.

There wasn't really anything special about Steve's office except for the fact that it fed his ego. It was in the corner and offered a nice view of the skyline. Beyond that it was decorated much like any other successful advisor's office. The wall behind Steve's desk was adorned with awards. Instead of books, his shelves held trophies celebrating his personal achievements. It was almost like an altar. In fact, Lucy had always joked that his office was a shrine to Saint Steve of Outlier Capital.

Another wall had some stock photography with motivational quotes. The wall directly in front of his desk held some beautiful photographs of his family. Below them was his liquor cabinet. He couldn't wait to sip on a nice, neatly poured glass of bourbon.

"It's a two-finger kind of night," Steve said to himself.

He started to reach for the bottle, when his phone rang.

"Who the heck is calling me at this hour?"

Steve considered ignoring it. But against his better judgement, picked up the phone.

"Thanks for calling Outlier Capital, this is Steve. How may I help you?"

"Um, Steve, it's Gerald."

Gerald was Steve's largest client. Steve had benefited greatly from Gerald's business. For that matter, so had Outlier Capital, but what really set Gerald apart was the fact Steve considered him a friend and a mentor.

In the early days of their professional relationship, they spent many hours talking about purpose and mission. But, over the last year, the relationship had become strained.

"I wasn't expecting you to pick up," Gerald continued. "Why are you at the office anyway? You should be home with Lucy and the kids."

"Oh hey, Gerald. Yeah, I finished dinner with the family and decided to come back into the office to work on a couple projects. In fact, I was looking over your account," Steve lied while tucking the phone into his neck and logging into his computer.

Steve stole a quick glance at the bottle of bourbon and decided he should wait to pour himself a glass.

"I was planning on leaving you a voicemail, but that's actually what I wanted to talk to you about."

There was something different in the tone of Gerald's voice. A lump formed in Steve's throat. He realized this call was probably not going to end up working in his favor.

"Great. What are your questions?" Steve asked, faking confidence. "By the way, you can always call my cell. You're more likely to get a hold of me."

"Well, I guess there is no easy way to do this," Gerald started, "but Norma and I have decided to make some changes to our investment strategy."

"Okay," said Steve. "Let's set up a time to meet and review the changes you would like to make."

"That won't be necessary," continued Gerald. "We've met with another advisor and they've already sent in the paperwork."

"Wait, what?" Steve stammered. "Another advisor? Here at Outlier?

"No," said Gerald. "And I'd rather not say."

"Well, how much are you talking about moving?"

Gerald sighed and said, "All of it."

Steve collapsed into his chair and now the lump in his throat had grown so big that it felt like his entire stomach was trying to crawl out through his mouth.

"And you were planning on delivering this news via my voicemail?" Steve demanded. "I wouldn't have expected that from you."

"Don't get defensive, Steve. I was going to ask you to give me a call in the morning. I have your cell phone, but given the hour I didn't want to bug you at home. If it makes any difference, we're not investing in the market."

Steve was speechless.

"Thanks for the update, Gerald, but no it doesn't make any difference. I'm having a difficult time processing the fact you and Norma made these changes without consulting with me. I don't understand. But my office will do our best to help facilitate the transfer in a timely and orderly fashion. Will there be anything else?"

"We are worried about you, Steve," said Gerald. "You're in terrible shape and your emotions are getting ahead of you. It's one of the reasons we are moving. Consider talking to someone, will you. It might be helpful."

"Well, Gerald," Steve said sarcastically, "I'll take that under advisement. Please give my best to Norma. Good night."

Steve waited until he heard the dial tone and then slammed his phone down on his desk. With both hands pressed firmly into this desk, he tried to make sense of what happened.

"Am I doing anything right?" Steve asked an empty room.

At his wits' end, Steve stormed across the room, grabbed the bottle of bourbon off the table, poured himself a full glass and chugged it.

Generally speaking, this was the type of bourbon that one would sip relaxingly, but Steve decided it was no longer a two-finger kind of night. He instead decided it had become a get-drunk-and-sleep-at-the-office kind of night.

He finished half of his second glass while staring out his office window. He continued pondering all that had happened in the last couple years. He saw his reflection and didn't recognize the man staring back at him. And then, it hit him like a ton of bricks—his marriage, his mission, his health, his relationship with God and his kids, even his relationship with his clients—he had allowed all of it to fall into disarray. He was tired, stressed and now he was pissed! Pissed at himself, at his wife and his clients. He was pissed with the world, really. It felt like everyone and everything had turned against him.

Steve gripped his glass harder. Without thinking, he turned and threw the glass at the wall as hard as he could. The sound of splintering glass snapped him out of his rage. He realized that he had thrown his glass into what used to be his most prized possession, a beautifully framed picture of his family. Not one of those cheesy, posed ones where everyone is wearing matching outfits, but a goofy photo that clearly demonstrated their true personalities and the love that they all shared.

Steve walked over to the picture that was now on the ground and just stared at the mess that he made.

As he knelt down to pick up the pieces, that lump in his throat reemerged. This time it continued to grow and within a few seconds, it felt like a Mack Truck had hit him in the chest. His vision blurred, his ears started ringing and his head throbbed with pain. Steve didn't know what was happening, but he knew that something was terribly wrong. He needed help.

But the only person he saw in the office was The Janitor.

Is he even still here? Steve wondered.

Steve began to think about Lucy and the girls. He tried to gather as much strength as possible as he stumbled out of his office toward the lobby. He was sorry he had been absent so much in the past couple years and regrets flooded his brain.

How many experiences did I miss?
Will they be okay without me?
Will the girls even remember me?
I can't believe I made them cry.
I hope they forgive me.

But before he could make it out his door or yell for help, Steve collapsed and everything went black.

WAKING UP

The roar of thunder and the sound of rain slamming against the window stirred Steve back to consciousness.

At first, he was not sure of where he was. His last memory was stumbling to his office door and praying that Lucy and the kids would be okay. As he looked around the room, he saw all the telltale signs that he was in the hospital. The typical IV drip going into his arm. The monitor making the typical noises. The bed with the typical bluish gray bedding. The chart hanging on the typical, over-sized hospital room door. Typically, one would be relieved to be alive but not Steve.

It's not that he wished to be dead, it's just that at that particular moment he didn't really feel anything. Then directly in front of him he saw six faces. Not human faces, but the Face Pain Scale that adorn the walls of just about every hospital room in America. It was as if they were mocking him. Steve recalled the last time he had seen those faces was when Lucy was in labor with their daughter, Elle. He smiled as he remembered trying to replicate those faces to help take Lucy's mind off of her labor pains. Those were different times—happier times.

Just then a nurse walked in, took a quick look at Steve's vital signs, made some notes, and walked out without even noticing he was awake. He was dazed and extremely fatigued, so he was fine remaining invisible for a moment longer. He hadn't even made an effort to let her know he was awake.

Steve continued to stare at those six faces and began to think about what happened. His emotions oscillated between gratitude, bitterness and self-pity.

A list of questions kept popping into his mind:

Why me?
How did I let this happen?
How could Gerald do this to me?
Were Lucy and the kids concerned about me?
Why wasn't Lucy here?
What am I going to do now?
Did I humiliate myself?
What next?

His thoughts were interrupted by an obnoxious beeping noise—an alarm alerting the medical staff that his blood pressure was elevated.

The same nurse came rushing in to turn the alarm off. This time she acknowledged that he was awake.

"Hello, honey," said the nurse. "Glad you're up. You're lucky to be alive, you know!"

"What do you mean?"

"Well, you had a heart attack, Sugar. If it weren't for The Janitor who was working late, you might not be here."

Steve recalled one of his last thoughts was whether The Janitor was still in the office.

"Yup, he was about to head out when he heard some commotion in your office. By the time he got there, you had collapsed."

"My wife. Does she know where I am?"

"She's been here since you arrived and hasn't left your side. Your friend, Gerald, came in for a while too, but your wife went home a few hours ago to get some rest. Doctor's orders. Speaking of the doctor, I'm going to go let him know that you're awake."

Steve was so groggy that he almost missed the fact that the nurse mentioned Gerald's name.

"Anything else, Sugar?"

"Can you call my wife and let her know I am awake? And if Gerald calls or stops by, I do not want to see him. Please make sure everyone knows that."

"If that's what you want, Darlin'."

Darlin'? Who's she calling "Darlin"? Steve thought as he drifted off to sleep.

After what felt like only a couple of minutes, Steve woke to the feeling of someone taking a hold of his hand. Not in an aggressive way, but in a soft, nurturing way. As he opened his eyes, Lucy's beautiful face came into focus.

Her eyes welled with tears and she said, "I am my beloved's."

Steve looked at her with a smile and felt grateful, a sensation he had not embraced in a very long time.

"And my beloved is mine," he replied with a faint smile. "It's been a while since we've said those words."

They both let out a nervous chuckle.

"How long was I asleep?"

"At least a couple hours. How do you feel?"

"Like all my clients lined up and hit me with a baseball bat a few times," said Steve as he tried to adjust his position and sit up on the bed.

"I have so many questions. Do you know how lucky you are? How lucky we are? If it weren't for The Janitor," Lucy said as she began to cry again.

Steve didn't really know how to respond.

As Lucy wiped away her tears, she said, "Gerald has been in to see you."

"I do not want to see or talk to him. How did he even know I was here?"

"I called him to tell him what happened. He told me about your conversation." Lucy hesitated before asking, "Do you want to talk about it?"

"No! I don't want to talk about it. I'm not ready to talk about it. Right now, all I want to do is go home. Can you find a doctor and figure out when we can get out of here?"

"Okay, I will go see if we can get the doctor to come in and fill us in with some details.

Lucy stopped short of the door and looked back at Steve.

"I need you to know something. We've struggled the past few months, but I am your number one fan. I will be ready to listen when you are ready to talk. And no matter what, I love you and I'm always in your corner."

A few minutes later Lucy walked back in with a doctor who pulled a stool up to Steve's bed, sat down and started to say, "You know—"

"Yes," interrupted Steve. "I'm lucky to be alive, The Janitor, yada, yada yada. Listen, Doc. I just want to get home. Can we make that happen?"

The doctor paused and looked at Lucy before responding.

"Actually, I was *going* to say that all things considered your heart is pretty strong and that we plan to keep you another night for observation, but if all goes well you can go home tomorrow."

"Great," said Steve without skipping a beat. "And what does the recovery look like?"

"Why don't you move over here?" the doctor said to Lucy so he could see her and Steve. "A full recovery, to the point when you can resume your normal activities, can take upward of three months. Rest will be an important factor in the recovery process as will some lifestyle changes. Because you had been somewhat active in the past and you have a supportive family, your recovery will likely be on the shorter end, but no promises."

"What kind of lifestyle changes?"

"Managing your blood pressure, eating a heart healthy diet, building exercise back into your routine, and avoiding stress. All of this will be medically supervised to eliminate any guess work."

Steve thought to himself, *Does this guy know what I do for a living? The only "healthy" thing I eat right now is a healthy dose of stress for breakfast. Sheesh! Avoid stress. What a joke!*

"Okay, Doc. Next question."

Steve paused and looked at Lucy.

"How soon can we have sex?"

"Steven!" Lucy said as she slapped him on the shoulder.

"Well, it's obvious that you're feeling better," said the doctor with a laugh. "We usually don't get that question for a few more weeks. That being said, probably best to wait a month before resuming any kind of sexual activity. And, in case you were wondering, that particular activity will not be supervised."

They had a good laugh, and the doctor stood up and left the room.

THE RECOVERY

As the weeks went by, Steve focused on his recovery and his family. He regained a significant amount of strength and stamina. His relationship with Lucy and the girls had improved dramatically as a simple byproduct of being present. This is something that did not go unnoticed or unappreciated by Lucy or his daughters.

And still, he felt mentally, emotionally and spiritually drained. He doubted whether he could resume his role at Outlier Capital.

Every time he thought about going back to work, he was overwhelmed by the idea of rebuilding. And more importantly, there was the unresolved matter of his relationship with Gerald.

Gerald had been reaching out to Steve on a regular, sometimes daily, basis. Lucy knew how much Steve's relationship with Gerald had meant to him, so she encouraged him to take his call, but time and again Steve ignored him. After all, Gerald was the one responsible for this mess. At least that is what Steve liked to tell himself.

Just then, Steve's cell phone began to ring. He saw that it was Gerald again and moved to ignore the call, but before he could touch his phone, Lucy grabbed it from the counter.

"What are you doing?" Steve shouted. "Don't you dare answer that call!"

"Steve," Lucy said calmly. "I am tired of seeing you this way. You need to talk to him. It's the only way to move forward."

"What would you like me to say to him, then, huh?" asked Steve. "It's his fault that I had this heart attack. If it weren't for him bailing on me, I'd probably be in my office doing my thing right now."

The phone was still buzzing in Lucy's hand.

"Well, if 'doing your thing' is being miserable and making us miserable, then I am glad he left you. If there is a silver lining to you having a heart attack—it is the fact that our relationship is better than it's been in years and you're making memories with the girls."

Lucy answered the phone.

"Hello, Gerald?"

"Well hello, Lucy. I didn't expect to hear your voice," Gerald said sheepishly. "Actually, I didn't really expect to hear anyone's voice. How are you and the girls?"

"Oh, we are doing well. We've enjoyed taking care of Steve and having him around the house. Thanks for asking! I assume you are calling for him?"

"You assume correctly," Gerald replied. "Is he up for talking?"

Lucy looked up at Steve. With arms crossed and a stern look on his face, he was shaking his head.

She smiled at him and said, "Absolutely. He's right here. Just a moment." And then she handed the phone to Steve and walked out of the room.

"Unbelievable," Steve mumbled.

Not sure what to say, he stood there staring at the phone. He wanted to give Gerald an earful, but instead he took a deep breath and restrained himself.

"I don't have much to say to you right now, Gerald," Steve sighed.

"Listen, Steve," said Gerald. "I know you are upset with me and when you are ready, we can sit down and talk about it, but that is not why I am calling."

"Why are you calling then?"

"Well, The Janitor has been asking about you and would like to meet with you."

"The Janitor? How do you know him and why would he want to meet me? His employer want a photo op or something? 'Local Janitor Saves Frustrated Businessman from Dying'."

"Steve, sarcasm does not look good on you. Just listen a minute, will you?"

"Okay, you're right. It's not my best quality. So how do you know him?"

"I will let him share the details, but The Janitor used to take care of one of my properties years ago and I got to know him pretty well. We ended up becoming friends and meet up for coffee every week."

"Wait, you have coffee with your janitor?"

"He's is much more than a janitor," said Gerald. "He's a friend. Anyway, we were having coffee and he told me how he was working late at one of his buildings and he saved some guy from dying from a heart attack. And I realized he was talking about you."

Steve was genuinely surprised. "Wow, small world."

"Sure is," said Gerald. "Well, what do you say?"

"About?"

"Meeting The Janitor. I am sure you will learn something and maybe make a new friend."

Steve paused for a few seconds to think about it. There was an enthusiasm in Gerald's tone that made Steve curious.

"Fine," said Steve. "The least I can do is say thank you."

"Excellent," declared Gerald. "He's free this Monday at noon. Does that work for you?"

"I'll have to check with Lucy, but I don't think that will be a problem," said Steve. "Where are we meeting?"

"Well, his main office happens to be in your building," replied Gerald. "I will call and let them know you will be there at noon on Monday."

Steve agreed to meeting on Monday a little too soon. He had been medically released to do almost everything he did before the heart attack, except for drive by himself. When Monday came around he asked Lucy if she would come with him, but Lucy had already made plans for a play date across town and couldn't reschedule.

Initially, Steve was annoyed that Lucy wouldn't adjust her plans, but the more he thought about it the more excited he got. This would be the first time in at least a month that he would venture out on his own.

As the Uber driver approached the building, Steve had a somewhat embarrassing revelation. In all the years he had worked at Outlier Capital, he had never entered the building through the first-floor lobby. He had always gone straight from the garage to the fortieth floor.

He had never said hello to the people that greeted his clients and guided them to the elevator bank or met the security guards who made sure no riff-raff was allowed in the building. He didn't know their names or their stories.

Steve wasn't clear why, but he became acutely aware that this attitude of his had really screwed things up.

At that moment, Steve's heart and mind began to open up like a parachute.

Part 2
STORY

THE JANITOR

With a fresh set of eyes and an open mind, Steve walked into the building and paused for a few moments, observing all the people coming and going. People were definitely in a hurry to get to their destination, but there was something different about the environment.

At first, Steve could not figure it out but then he saw it. The entire lobby staff was smiling and greeting people as they entered and left the building, and the people resounded with smiles too. It was contagious. It may seem simple, but it struck him at the core and he began to smile.

Then a gigantic security guard approached Steve with an equally gigantic grin.

"Hello, sir. May I help guide you to your destination today?"

"Um yeah. I am here to see The Janitor."

"Well, that sounds exciting," said the security guard. "You're in for a real treat. He's a special guy."

Steve gave the security guard a confused look. He didn't understand why everyone was making a fuss about a guy who sweeps the floors and picks up the trash.

"Follow me, and I will take you to his elevator."

Steve entered the elevator and it was unlike any elevator he had ever been in. It only had one button. He had seen the maintenance crews' offices in the parking garage, so when he pushed the button he expected to feel the sensation of descending to the garage level, but that is not what happened. In fact, nothing happened.

The elevator doors opened back up and the gigantic security guard was standing there again with his equally gigantic grin.

"My apologies, sir. I forgot to swipe the keycard. You should be squared away now. Go ahead and push the button again."

As soon as the doors closed, the elevator began to go up and not down as was expected. Steve was thoroughly confused. He could feel his heart rate elevating, so he closed his eyes and took some deep breaths.

A few moments later the elevator doors opened and Steve stepped into the most magnificent office he had ever seen. He was positive that he was in the wrong place. Without even realizing it, he walked over to take in the view of the skyline. The exterior walls to the office consisted of floor-to-ceiling windows that were so clear it was like they weren't there.

He had never seen the city from this height before and it was breathtaking. As Steve began to scan the rest of the office, he noticed there were photographs of people everywhere. Some he recognized as celebrities or athletes and some well-known business tycoons while others he didn't recognize at all.

There was one picture, however, that stood out to him. It was a picture of Gerald and Norma with The Janitor.

What the heck is going on here? Steve wondered.

The suddenly he heard the sound of a toilet flushing and Steve looked over as the door swung open.

"Um, I'm sorry. I must be in the wrong place. Maybe I got in the wrong elevator?"

"Nope," The Janitor replied as he was drying his hands. "You're definitely in the right place. Gerald told me you would be swinging by around lunchtime today."

The Janitor walked toward Steve with his arm outstretched.

Steve immediately recognized the man's face as the one he saw the night of his heart attack. But instead of wearing a janitor's uniform, the man walking toward him was impeccably dressed.

"You're The Janitor?" Steve asked dumbfounded as he shook his hand.

"Well, that's what people call me. Tell you what, I don't know about you, but I am hungry. I didn't know what you liked or disliked so I had my team prepare a variety of food for us to share, including my favorite: peanut butter and jelly sandwiches. We can have something to eat and I will share with you what is going on."

Steve and The Janitor sat at a small table dipping their peanut butter and jelly sandwiches in milk without saying a word. Steve was still feeling bewildered. He didn't know where this conversation would take him, but he was certainly growing more curious by the minute.

Steve started to chuckle a little.

"What is it?" asked The Janitor.

"I just think it is a little funny that here we are in this amazing office, overlooking this beautiful city, eating peanut butter sandwiches and milk."

The Janitor simply smiled as he took another bite from his soggy sandwich. "You must have a lot of questions. Where would you like to sta−?"

"How did you meet, Gerald?" Steve interrupted.

"In a similar way to how I met you."

"Saved his life too, huh?" asked Steve sarcastically.

"No. Actually, I met him at one of the offices I was cleaning. In fact, it was a building he just purchased from me, but he didn't know that at the time. He just figured I was part of the cleaning crew. Sound familiar?"

Steve looked down at the coffee table in embarrassment.

"Let me back up and tell you a little bit more about me and the history of this company. But first, I need to get another sandwich. They're delicious, aren't they?"

The Janitor stood up and walked over to the display of food and refilled his milk. He paused and pointed to the photographs hanging on the wall. "You see the people in these pictures? Some of them you might recognize, but others are completely unfamiliar. Well, each of these photographs was taken after some event that impacted our lives. Some were taken after we entered into a mutually beneficial partnership or closed some kind of a deal, while others were taken at a special dinner or fun event. The bottom line is I consider them all family. I would do anything for them."

Must be nice, Steve thought to himself as he looked at the wall and lusted after the wealth the people in those images held.

"We are going to talk more about these folks, and you may even meet a couple, but their success, at least the things most people associate with success, didn't have much to do with us working together."

ANGELICA

The Janitor sat back down at the table with another plate of peanut butter and jelly sandwiches to share. "You see that big picture in the center? Ain't she a beauty? That's my wife, Angelica, and when she started this company 45 years..."

"Your wife started this company?" Steve interrupted. "And 45 years ago! I imagine there weren't too many women-owned business back then."

"It was certainly tough, but she was tough right back. In fact, she was a quarter Sicilian, so she had that going for her, too," he laughed. "Anyway, she had one core value that she operated the company by: see people as people first, not as opportunities to make a buck or get rich."

"Was?"

"Yeah," The Janitor sighed. "Ten years into the business, she passed away unexpectedly."

"I'm sorry to hear that," said Steve. "I can only imagine how much you miss her."

"I miss her terribly every day." The Janitor took a deep breath as he choked up.

"You see, I was working, too. But I was in a much different space mentally, emotionally, spiritually," The

Janitor continued. "I was an advertising manager. And let me tell you something in case you didn't know. In that business, everyone and everything is a walking dollar sign. Merely a means to an end."

The Janitor stood up and walked over to the picture of Angelica and stood there quietly staring at her with his hands in his pockets. "She worked hard, but I had no idea just how hard. This little janitorial company of hers grew and grew and grew. I was blown away by how she handled it all. The success and the failures. The company even started to purchase and manage properties. I remember times when she would come home upset. Not because of the normal wear and tear of running a business but because her employees were experiencing challenges in their own lives. It always baffled me how much she could care, but that's how she was."

The Janitor poured himself another glass of milk and returned to the table. "Whenever she encountered an obstacle or was rejected, she would confidently smile and say we will build a relationship and find a way. I mean, Steve, who says that? It was astonishing."

"Sounds unbelievable."

"And sometimes," The Janitor said with half a smile, "it was annoying. She was positive nearly all the time. Until the day she died, I never really understood how she could deal with it all."

Just then an intercom rang.

"Pardon the interruption, but I just wanted you to know that your 2 p.m. appointment called to reschedule."

"No pardon needed. I had completely lost track of time here with my new friend," The Janitor hollered back. "Thanks for the update! I don't think I have anything after that but just in case can you block out the rest of my day, please?

"My pleasure," replied the office manager.

"My, time flies when you're having fun and sharing stories. How are you doing for time, Steve?

"Well, I told my wife that I would be gone all afternoon, but let me send her a text to let her know I'm okay."

Steve took out his phone and there were several text messages from Lucy. "Um, this might take a minute," Steve said.

"Thought I heard a lot of buzzing. Take all the time you need."

How's it going?

Just talked to Gerald.

The Janitor isn't really a janitor.

What's he like?

Can't wait to hear about it!!

Call me!! Love you!

Kind of mind blowing.

Not sure where we're going...

He's sharing a ton... too much? I actually FEEL something for the first time in awhile...

I know it might hurt to hear that... I've never stopped loving you and the girls...

Not hurt. Love you, too.

Looking forward to the future.

I'm sure he's sharing for a reason. Roll with it.

Have you eaten?

Call me when you're done.

Yup. He brought up PB&Js

I've had like three

Even dipped them in milk.

Will call you when finished...

"I'm good to go," Steve said as he put his phone away.

"Like I was saying," The Janitor continued. "I never really understood my wife until after she died. To this day, I still fight with regret. Week after week, her customers came knocking on my door. They would tell me stories about things she had done for them. One guy told me about a time when he asked her why she loved picking up other people's trash so much. And you know what she said, Steve?"

"No idea. Something about her people or serving her customers?"

"Nope!" said The Janitor. "She told this guy that she didn't see it as picking up trash. She saw it as clearing a path for the future. Isn't that something?"

"I suppose that's one way of looking at it."

The Janitor stood up and walked back to Angelica's picture. "I had been too busy making a buck to see it. And I was sure, if I missed it then most everyone else was probably missing it, too."

"Forgive me, but what were you missing, exactly?"

"It's so subtle," replied The Janitor. "So much so that it often eludes even the most thoughtful people. You see, Steve, the thing I was missing is the fact that we alone control the definition of our self-worth. I'm not sure if Angelica was aware that she had defined it for herself, but she sure lived each day that way. It was like someone turned the lights on in my head and I realized I wanted to live that way, too. So I quit my job the next day and took over the company with the idea of adding what little I could to what Angelica started. And that brings us back to how I met Gerald."

"Let me guess," said Steve. "He was the guy who asked Angelica about picking up other people's trash?"

"Bingo," said The Janitor. "After taking over the company, I found myself a little bit strapped for cash, so I had to sell one of our properties. Fortunately, Gerald was one of our tenants and he was interested in buying the building for his own company. We had never met before and I was there cleaning things the night before the deal closed when we bumped into each other. I introduced myself as Angelica's husband. He immediately started to tell me about what a huge fan of hers he was. And that the comment she made about clearing a path for the future changed the entire way he worked with his own employees and customers."

"Wow," remarked Steve. "You never know who you're going to meet. For the most part, I've only known Gerald to ever be a thoughtful and generous person."

There was a momentary pause as they both reflected on the conversation they've had. It stirred up so many emotions in both of them: joy, fear, gratitude among them.

"Why were you there cleaning the building?" asked Steve. "You had employees still, right?"

"Sure. I still clean buildings from time to time. It's simply a time when I feel I can still connect with Angelica. There aren't any distractions or interruptions and I can share with her what's going on in my head and heart. And do you want to know the best part, Steve?

"What's that?"

"All she can do is listen." The Janitor continued to say between laughing and looking up at the ceiling as if he could see Angelica looking down on him with an unimpressed look on her face. "It's also during those times when I get my best ideas. Come to think of it, I'm overdue for some time with Angelica. Can we continue the conversation another day?"

"I'd love to," Steve said finishing his glass of milk.

"Great, because I've really enjoyed spending time with you," said The Janitor. "I have a pretty full schedule the rest of this week but I don't work on Fridays. We can meet at my home; same time?"

"I'm sure I can make that work."

"Excellent. Here's my address," The Janitor said as he scribbled on to a piece of scrap paper. "Need to call your wife?"

"Oh yes. I will text her," Steve replied as he looked at the address. He immediately recognized the location. It was just outside the city limits and one of the most prestigious neighborhoods in the area. Lots of money there. He could not wait to see what kind of house The Janitor lived in. He was sure it must be magnificent.

The Janitor walked with Steve to the elevator. As the doors opened, The Janitor placed his hand on Steve's shoulder.

"Go home and love your wife today," The Janitor said with a tear in his eye. "We will continue this on Friday."

Twenty minutes later Steve jumped into the car with Lucy. As she drove away, he looked at the building and began to process what had just transpired over the last couple of hours. Then, he looked at her and smiled, but didn't say anything.

"You're awfully quiet. You can't keep me in suspense forever," Lucy said through a nervous chuckle. "What's he lke? What did you talk about?"

"Did you know that his wife started the janitorial company?" Steve asked.

"Not until Gerald told me this afternoon," replied Lucy. "What a remarkable woman she must have been."

"Yeah, some of the stories he shared with me were pretty powerful. I'm still processing them. And Lucy?"

"Yes?"

"I love you."

Lucy's lip began to quiver. "I love you, too."

Steve took Lucy's hand and placed it in his and rested them both on his lap. "One more thing. I'll know more when we meet again on Friday, but I think he is going to mentor me and maybe introduce me to some people."

Lucy squeezed his hand tight. "I believe in you and it sounds like he sees something in you, too."

THE CHOICE

By Thursday night, Steve was so anxious that he could hardly sleep. There was something about The Janitor. And for the life of him, Steve could not quite figure it out. Why was he interested in helping Steve or anyone else for that matter? He didn't need to. After hours of tossing and turning, he grabbed his phone off the night stand.

"Ugh! 4:30 a.m.," Steve mumbled to himself. "What the heck am I going to do for the next five hours?"

Steve decided to head outside and left a note for Lucy:

Went for a walk.
Couldn't sleep.
Be back soon.

Moments later he was walking briskly up the sidewalk, completely lost in his thoughts.

Where did Angelica find the ability to define her sense of self-worth?
Was it possible in today's world to simply see people as people and still make money?

Who were all those people in The Janitor's pictures?
Am I going to meet any of them?
What is his house like? I bet it's huge.
What's up with the sandwiches?

A couple hours later Steve walked back into the house with some bagels and cream cheese. Lucy gave him an unimpressed look.

"Hey, it's low-fat cream cheese and I'll only eat half a bagel."

"Guess what?"

"I can have a whole bagel with real cream cheese?"

"Something even better," Lucy said with a smile. "The doctor's office just called and they said you are now cleared to drive by yourself."

In William Wallace fashion Steve threw his hands in the air and yelled, "FREEEDOMMMMM" at the top of his lungs.

Tina and Elle thought it was hilarious and burst out laughing and mimicking him.

"I suppose you won't need me to drive you then?" asked Lucy.

"I know you were looking forward to it, but I'd like to go by myself. Is that okay with you, Mommy?" Steve asked sarcastically as he winked at Lucy.

Her response was the all too familiar vicious eye roll and arm punch combo.

"Hey, no punching the patient."

Noon couldn't come fast enough. By 11:15, Steve hit the highway. He turned up the volume on his stereo and stepped on the gas. It felt great to be in control and to experience the thrill of power and speed again. And then it struck him: the last time he had driven on this highway was the night he nearly died. He let up off the gas, but continued to turn up the volume. He began to feel butterflies swooping back and forth in his stomach. The last time he felt that sensation was when he asked Lucy to marry him.

The GPS system brought Steve's thoughts back to the present as it alerted him of approaching his exit. He had always wanted a reason to drive through this neighborhood, but never did because he didn't want people to think he was a creep. This was his chance and as he turned the corner and his jaw dropped.

While the rest of the city was shrouded by sky-scrapers and the incessant honking of horns, this place was an oasis. The tree-lined streets and lus-cious landscaping alone made this neighborhood el-igible to be the most photographed places in the country. But the homes are what really pushed this place over the edge. From magnificent Mediter-raneans to charming bungalows and modern urban sanctuaries, each home was custom-built and most likely a personification of its owner's personality.

"Sheesh, these things are ridiculous," Steve chuck-led.

As he turned the corner at the end of the street, he saw The Janitor's home. It was a stunning Tudor style home, no doubt built by a master craftsman. It was more than a house but not quite a mansion and sat on at least an acre of beautifully manicured landscaping. From the little he knew of The Janitor's personality, he decided it fit him perfectly: refined, thoughtful, proud and yet somehow still humble.

Before Steve had even parked the car, The Janitor was standing on the porch waving enthusiastically.

As soon as Steve got out of the car The Janitor placed his hand on his shoulder and said, "Welcome! I'm glad you're here."

"Well, I am very much glad to be here. Thanks for the invitation."

The Janitor left his hand on Steve's shoulder and guided him into the formal living room of the home. The only things more astonishing than the incredible nine-foot-tall windows, vaulted ceilings and gigantic fireplace was the fact there were more pictures on the wall of people posing with The Janitor. The one that stood out this time was a picture of The Janitor and the Pope.

"Wait a second! You met the Pope?"

"I went on a pilgrimage to Rome and we were fortunate to have a private audience with him. Good guy."

"I would hope so," Steve laughed. "Who haven't you met?"

"I haven't met your wife," The Janitor replied with a mischievous grin.

"Well, we will have to fix that someday soon. I know she's dying to meet you."

"How about Sunday night? I am having a few friends over and I'd love to host you."

"That's very generous of you, but I don't want to impose. Besides, we won't even know anyone."

"You won't be imposing and come Sunday you'll know everyone in the room."

"Wait, what do you mean?"

"You'll see."

The Janitor stood up and walked into the adjacent dining room and returned with a tray full of peanut butter and jelly sandwiches and milk.

Steve started to chuckle.

"What's so funny?"

"Is there a story behind your affection for PB & Js?"

"When Angelica and I first got married we didn't have much, especially when she started the business. To save money we would eat peanut butter and jelly sandwiches with milk and sticky white bread. The kind that would stick to the roof of your mouth. Back then they were just cheap, easy, and functional. Now every time I make one, I think about her," The Janitor concluded as he dipped his sandwich into the glass of milk.

Steve sat quietly, taking a bite of his sandwich, too, and made a mental note that he really needed to step up his game with Lucy. What simple things would make him remember her if something happened or vice versa? He wasn't sure and it bothered him.

"So listen," began The Janitor. "After you left, I went to clean some offices and talk with Angelica like I do. I was telling her about you and how we met, when a couple things about that office struck me. First off, it was one of those start up companies and they didn't actually have any offices inside."

"What do you mean?" Steve asked.

"You know, offices like the one you have and I have," The Janitor continued. "With doors and walls. They didn't have them. I just was amazed and wondered how the heck they could focus."

"Ah, yeah. The open floor plan. They're kind of a thing right now."

"The other thing I noticed were the motivational quotes and inspirational messages written all over the place: walls, desks and there were even a few on the floor. Everywhere. Motivational books, too."

The Janitor took another bite of his soggy PB & J.

"You know how I told you I get my best ideas when I'm cleaning?"

"Sure," Steve said as he reached for his glass to wash down a mouthful of sandwich.

"Two things hit me, and I think they might be helpful."

"I'm all ears," Steve said as he leaned in.

"Everyone—you, me, my employees, your clients and even my nosy neighbors—everyone wants to perform at our full potential."

"Okay."

"We are all in the hunt. Most spend a ridiculous amount of time reading motivational books and inspirational quotes hoping that one day this elusive, mythical creature will appear one day and reveal the truth of who they are, you know, in a Chronicles of Narnia kind of way."

"Interesting. I've never thought of it that way."

"I know," The Janitor said through a smile filled with PB & J. "That's just it. No one is thinking about it. The reality is each of us is already in possession of the key needed to free our potential, but it's up to us to master the pieces. That's the first thing."

"Pieces? Like a puzzle?"

"Yup. One key made of four pieces and it won't function properly without all of them."

"So what are the pieces?"

"We'll get there in a minute."

"What's the second idea?"

"The second is even bigger than the first," The Janitor continued. "There's all this stuff about 'starting with why' or 'finding your why,' but it all begins with believing you are worthy of a why in the first place."

Now ever since meeting The Janitor, Steve had only felt like his life was going to change, but as of that moment he was absolutely positive it would. Never in his life had Steve stopped to consider the idea that he was worthy of anything let alone a "why." He just did what he thought needed to be done and that was that, but this idea of being worthy struck him to his core. He desperately wanted to be worthy of a why. But he was still skeptical.

"Okay, let's say I agree with you. How does one put the pieces together so they can use it, or master it or whatever?

"Now that is a good question," said The Janitor. "But I'm afraid you're not going to like the answer."

"Try me."

"I believe the great Lou Holtz said it best when he told me there are roughly 422,000 words in our vocabulary, and the most important word among them is the word 'choice.' You decide to, Steve. It's that simple."

"You're right, I don't like it."

"The first piece of the key, to believing you are worthy, is choosing to master your story."

"What about it?

"All of us have the opportunity to direct the narrative of our life, regardless of our circumstances."

"It can't be that simple."

"Why not? You've got to choose something, don't you? Right now, you're choosing not to believe in the simplicity of the idea. It may be a default choice, but it is still a choice and one that blinds you from seeing what is possible. Let me ask you a question, if I gave you some complicated formula or technique would it make it easier for you to believe?"

In the past, Steve had looked at new ideas with an open mind, but after years of disappointment, he had lost his sense of optimism and had grown cynical. This new journey of his was requiring a great deal of mental fortitude.

"And remember, it's just the first piece."

THE WINE CELLAR

Steve grabbed a couch pillow, hugged it close to his chest and leaned back into the cushions, reflecting on the question The Janitor just presented to him. "Could it really be so simple?"

"Comfortable, are you?"

The Janitor got up and walked into the kitchen leaving Steve on the couch.

"Hey, Steve!" yelled the Janitor from the kitchen.

"Yeah," Steve replied, lost in his own thoughts.

"The cave you fear to enter is where the treasure lies!"

"What does that mean?"

Steve jumped off the couch and headed into the kitchen, but the Janitor wasn't there.

"The cave you fear to enter is where the treasure lies. It's a quote from an author named Joseph Campbell," The Janitor shouted. "I read it in one of those motivational books in that office I was telling you about. Come over here, I want to show you something I think will help paint the picture."

Steve followed the sound of the Janitor's voice only to discover him standing in front of a door behind a cleverly designed false wall.

"I bet this is the best hiding spot in the entire house."

The Janitor turned and looked directly at Steve.

"The cave you fear to enter..."

"Is where the treasure lies," Steve finished. "I don't really understand what that means but I assume there is a cave with some treasure in it behind this door?"

"Oh, most definitely," said the Janitor. "Most definitely."

"Stay here a moment while I go down and turn the lights on." The Janitor opened the door and descended into the darkness. The lights turned on and The Janitor yelled, "Come on down."

Steve walked carefully down the spiral staircase which ended in The Janitor's wine cellar.

"Beautiful, isn't it?"

The only wine cellar Steve had ever been into was the one in his bedroom closet where he had about six bottles of wine on a cheap rack from Target. But when he stepped into The Janitor's cellar, he instantly felt like he was transported back in time. The walls consisted of worn out brick and mortar that looked like it had been pulled from some old church ruins.

As the walls stretched toward the ceiling, they began to form intricate arches that danced back and forth from one side of the cellar to the other. And instead of being lined with the more modern wine racks that Steve had seen in magazines, under the arches were six colossal bookshelves that were easily as old as the walls behind them. And resting on the shelves were what must have been thousands of bottles of wine, most covered in a thin layer of dust. It was unlike anything Steve had ever seen.

"I don't have many possessions that I hold dear beside my house and my cars, which I guess is a lot actually, but I love my cellar. I modeled it after an old monastic library from late 1600s. So many stories down here. Each one different. In fact, that's why I have the wines on these bookshelves instead of racks. Each one of these bottles is a manuscript and has been on its own hero's journey. Do me a favor and grab a bottle off that shelf next to you."

A little uncertain on where The Janitor was going with this, Steve grabbed a bottle and handed it to The Janitor.

"Great choice, Steve. A fine vintage, and better yet one we won't need to decant."

"Let's see, where did I put that corkscrew?"

The Janitor reached into the shelf where Steve grabbed the bottle, retrieved a corkscrew, and began to open the wine.

"So you're probably wondering why I brought you down here," The Janitor said as he pulled the cork from the bottle.

"To drink wine?"

"Yes and no."

The Janitor briefly disappeared behind a corner, returned with two glasses and began to pour the wine.

"Adversity can produce great fruit," The Janitor said handing a glass to Steve. "Go ahead. Take a sip."

Steve did not consider himself a wine connoisseur by any stretch, but right now there was a genuine flavor explosion occurring in his mouth and he was positive this was by far the best wine he had ever tasted.

"What do you think?"

"The only word I can think of is remarkable, but it's much more than that."

"Wine is used to celebrate. Wine is used to honor. Wine is used to remember. Most people enjoy a glass or two of wine at dinner or while they're out at a party, but not many people take the time to consider what it took to get that wine from the vines and into the glass you're holding.

In fact, there are hundreds of variables that shape the wine inside these bottles and no two are alike. Everything from where the vines are planted, how old they are, the specific varietal, the rain, frost, heat, drought, wind, wars, earthquakes. Heck, even the wine maker's mood plays a role."

"Wars?"

"Absolutely, World War I, World War II. Much of the wine in this cellar comes from Europe. They may not have directly impacted the wine itself, but they definitely have played a role in the story around the wine. Most people want the immediate gratification of a buzz, but it is in the glory of the struggle that the characteristics, the things we actually enjoy about the wine, the things that make this wine remarkable, are born."

The Janitor paused to savor a sip from his own glass.

"Life is the same way, but unlike the grape, we get to decide, we get to choose, how we let the adversity or triumph that we experience affect and influence us. Is it happening to you or is it happening for you? Just take your heart attack for example."

"What about it?" asked Steve defensively.

"I don't mean to sound disingenuous, but did it happen to you or for you? What new things are possible because of it?"

"Well, I can assure you, it definitely happened to me. But I see what you're saying. It's up to me to decide what I do with it?"

"That's it. You're the winemaker. I said it was simple, but I didn't say it would be easy."

Steve saw a well-used, leather chair in the corner of the room and plopped down with a sigh.

"You know," Steve said before taking another sip of the remarkable wine in his glass. "I think I've done this before."

"Really?"

"Yeah, but it's pretty silly."

"Let's hear it." The Janitor said leaning against one of the massive bookshelves.

"My dad was an army officer and wasn't around as much as the other neighborhood dads. Don't get me wrong. He was a great dad and incredibly generous, but he was serving our country and was just gone a lot. But I was a kid and I couldn't comprehend that type of obligation or commitment. I just wanted him to be around, you know, like the other dads. But this one time when I was 12, he actually came home from work at the same time as my friends' dads. I was so excited. He walked in, gave my mom a kiss, tossed me a brand new football and said let's play catch. I bolted outside."

Steve took another sip from his glass.

"We were out in the front yard playing catch and I can remember feeling so happy. But then my mom came out. She said someone from the base was on the phone and needed to speak with him. My dad tossed me the ball and said, 'I'll be right back.'"

"Let me guess," said The Janitor. "He didn't come back out."

"Well, he came back out but jumped in his car and headed to base. It sucked and I bawled my eyes out. To this day, I don't know why he had to leave, but that night while I was going to sleep I concocted a story. I told myself that he had to leave to save the world or some ridiculous thing. It made me feel good and I guess it protected me from becoming too resentful."

Steve took a large sip, finishing off the wine his glass. "I've never shared that with anyone other than Lucy, but I supposed it's a cave with some treasure in it."

"Well, I'd say so. It is a great example of choosing to own your story and there definitely is a cache of treasure there worth more than the finest jewels. And Steve, part of owning your story is giving your-self the freedom to be emotional. That will become even more important as you explore other caves in your quest to uncover the hidden treasure within you. Is your dad still alive?"

"Yeah. My mom's been gone for a while, but my dad's still here. We're not very close. We see each other once or twice a year."

"Does he know you nearly died?"

"I don't think Lucy ever called. So how many caves are there?" Steve asked switching subjects.

"Considering that no two of us is alike, there will definitely be a wide variety and will require each of us to examine our hearts. But I think it is safe to say there are six that almost everyone needs to explore: faith, family, fitness, friends, finances and fun."

"Clever. All 'F's' makes it easy to remember."

"Whether it's the vineyard or the caves, the soil needs to be tended to, the weeds need to be pulled, some rocks may need to be removed, and some of the vines may need to be pruned. But the awesome thing is that as you explore, you get to decide what stays and what goes."

"So how do we begin?"

"Right where you are. Assess your current reality. What is going well? What is not going well? What do you like? What don't you like? What are the beliefs or activities keeping you stuck in your current reality? Truth is that all of us desire a better future than what we've got. It's just how we are wired. I would argue that anyone who says different isn't being honest with themselves."

"So we ask those questions for each of the six areas?"

"Absolutely; then you use the powerful brain God gave you and begin to forecast your future. What does your desired reality look like, feel like, smell like? What's going well? What are the beliefs, habits, actions you need to adopt in order to see the fruit of your desired reality?"

"And all these ideas just came to you the other night while you were cleaning?" Steve asked incredulously.

The Janitor shrugged his shoulders. "I suppose I've been thinking about these concepts for a while but, yes, they became clear the other night while I was cleaning. Wild, I know. But here's the icing on the cake, the real secret sauce. Ever hear of Jim Rohn?"

"He's the guy who said you're the average of the five people you spend the most time with, right?"

"Exactly, so let's take his advice and apply it to your desired reality in these six areas. Who are the five people in each of these areas who are already living your desired reality? How can you get them into your sphere of influence? Call 'em your 'future five.' We'll be talking about that at dinner on Sunday."

"Now that would be a game changer."

"More importantly, this work, and it is work, puts you in a position to master your gifts, your action and your community which are the three remaining pieces.

"Are you going to help me find those pieces, too?"

"Oh no," said The Janitor. "But come upstairs. I want to introduce you to the folks who will. Their pictures are hanging on the walls.

And with that, The Janitor bounced up the stairs with Steve right behind him.

THE GREATEST TREASURE

These are really my greatest treasure," The Janitor said pointing to the pictures on the walls in the living room. "These...and the ones hanging back in my office."

Steve stood in the center of the room, marveling at the faces in the pictures on the wall. There were men and women of all shape, sizes, and colors. Some were recognizable business tycoons, heads of state, or celebrities, but there were plenty of faces he had never seen until today. As he stood there wondering what their stories were, he couldn't help but feel a sense of wonder bubbling up inside.

Who will the next teacher be? he wondered quietly. And then it hit him, the one thing they all shared in common was The Janitor.

Just then The Janitor started giggling while singing, "*Make new friends, but keep the old. One is silver and the other's gold.*"

"Which one is he?" Steve laughed pointing to the picture of The Janitor and the Pope.

"What do you mean?"

"Silver or gold?"

"Are you kidding me?" The Janitor laughed. "He's got a direct line to the man upstairs. Definitely gold," he concluded with a wink. "Despite what that old nursery rhyme says, all my friends are like gold to me."

The Janitor walked over to his gigantic fireplace and pointed to a picture of a beautiful Asian woman holding a violin.

"This is Charlotte Cho, but her friends call her Chaz. If you met her ten years ago, you would never believe that she would become one of the world's most sought-after violinists and is headlining auditoriums and arenas around the globe."

"Really? How did you meet?"

"The short story is her family died in a tragic car accident and she came to live with her grandmother who happened to be an employee of mine."

"Woah!"

"It truly is a remarkable comeback story, but I don't want to steal her thunder so I'll let her fill in the blanks tonight."

"Sounds great—wait! Did you say tonight?"

"Yup. She's playing for a benefit concert at City Arena. Tonight is the show for family and friends. I've got an extra ticket. Think you can come?"

"I'll have to check with Lucy, but I think I can work it out."

"Great. Curtain call is at 7 p.m. So I will call Chaz and let her know that we will meet at 5 p.m. Should give us plenty of time to have a great conversation about gifts and then we can watch the magic happen."

The Janitor stood quietly staring at the faces on his wall and then looked at Steve.

"In fact, see if Lucy can spare you for part of the day tomorrow as well. I want to introduce you to Fidel Lopez," The Janitor said pointing to another picture.

Steve immediately recognized Fidel. He had been a mover and shaker in local real estate circles for years. He was well known for being an honest broker in what had become a slimy industry within the city.

"Recognize him?"

"Sure do. I've seen his face on some of the commercial real estate billboards around the city. Even heard him say once that his claim to fame was that he could outwork anyone in the business."

"Well, I'd say that is true. He's a phenomenal negotiator, but only because he is makes sure he is the most knowledgeable about what is at stake."

"How did you guys meet?"

"I met him in a town car."

"Oh, so you guys shared a ride?"

"Not exactly," said The Janitor. "He was my driver."

"Wait, he was your driver? There's gotta be more to the story."

"There is! And I'm going to leave you in suspense until you meet him," The Janitor said with a grin. "The story is so much more fun when we tell it together."

Steve walked over to the couch and sat down.

"Why are you doing all this for me?" Steve asked timidly. "I'm struggling with feeling worthy of all this. You're being so generous and I haven't done anything to deserve it."

"Honestly, I didn't know where our conversation would take us either, but I extended an invitation and you said yes. That was a good enough start for me," The Janitor said leaning against the massive fireplace. "Besides, you're human and it's normal for your brain to fight you when you're doing new and challenging things. It's a powerful organ, but it wants to keep you in the comfort zone. When you feel that way, go back to the first key and remind it who's boss. We good?"

"Yeah, we're good."

"Okay, so you're going to check in with Lucy about tonight and tomorrow. While you're at it, don't forget about Sunday."

"Sunday?"

"The dinner I mentioned. I am dying to meet your wife," The Janitor grinned. "And Chaz, Fidel, and Bill will be joining us as well."

"I'm pretty sure Lucy has you beat there," Steve smiled. "You guys can have a competition. Not sure you can top her excitement. I'll text her now."

"Great. While you're doing that I have to run to my study and make a note of something. Be right back."

Hey! How's it going?

More adventures with The Janitor.

Wants to intro me to some people

Things good here.

Miss you though.

Weird not having you here.

Been around so much lately.

Sounds fun though. When?

He wants to intro me to a music artist... tonight....

Tonight?

Who is it?

WIll you feel up for it?

Chaz Cho.

A performance violinist...

I'm feeling good....

Chaz Cho! Saw her on PBS... She's incredible! Let me know what she's like.

Who else?

A local bizman named Fidel. Tomorrow.

Wow.

He's really investing in you.

Kind of overwhelming.

By the way...

I won't have to tell you what Chaz is like...

You'll meet her on Sunday!

WHAT!?!?!?!?!

The Janitor is hosting a dinner

Invited us to join him.

She'll be there, too... Others too....

So exciting!

I will work on a sitter.

OMG! What should I wear...

Not too formal...

I'll confirm...

You okay with this??

YES!

As long as you're up for it...

I'm all in....

Okay... Stay tuned.

Love you....

"Get that permission slip signed?" The Janitor said as he walked back into the room.

"Yup. We're good to go on all fronts," Steve said, putting his phone away. "So who's Bill?"

"Bill Cooper is a personal development coach. Most of his clients are executives, athletes and celebrities. He works with all kinds of people."

"Which picture is his?" Steve asked looking at the wall of fame.

"His is on the wall at my office."

"So far there's been a story behind how you met Chaz and Fidel. How did you meet Bill?"

The Janitor sat down on the couch across from Steve and looked out at his beautifully manicured yard.

"When I decided to carry on Angelica's legacy and lead this company, I struggled keeping it all together."

"As in the company itself?" Steve interrupted.

"No, as in my life! I was a mess; I was burning out fast. I knew that if things didn't change, I was going down and I would take the company with me. I started attending conferences of all types to expand my thinking—personally and professionally. Bill spoke at one of the sessions and I hired him immediately to coach me. He's been one of my closet friends ever since. In fact, he was actually the guy who organized the trip to Rome where we met the Pope."

Steve got up to take a closer look at the picture of The Janitor and the Pope.

"Too bad the Pope's busy."

"Bill's a good substitute teacher," The Janitor joked. "He's an expert on the topic of friendship and community."

"I could certainly use more of both."

The Janitor stole a quick look at the grandfather clock in the corner.

"Speaking of friends," The Janitor said as he stood and walked toward Steve. "We've only got a few hours before we met up with Chaz. Why don't you head home and get some rest."

"Good idea," Steve said. "Where should I meet you?"

"Let's plan on meeting in the lobby of City Arena at 4:45 p.m. Sound good?"

"Sounds great," Steve replied as they walked toward the front door. "And thank you for today, for sharing your wisdom, your home, and your greatest treasures with me. It's an example I intend to live up to."

The Janitor stopped just short of the door and reached his hand into the drawer of a beautiful credenza in the entryway. When his hand returned he was holding a leather-bound book.

"This is a new beginning," The Janitor said placing is hand on Steve's shoulder. "I thought you might want to jot down some of your thoughts and breakthroughs."

"I've never been much of a writer, but I think this is a perfect time to begin. See you soon."

Steve pulled slowly out of The Janitor's driveway and continued home in the quiet, reflecting on all that had taken place. He was overcome with feelings of immense gratitude.

Reflect and Respond

Thoughts from Steve's Journal

Some say that we are simply the sum of our experiences and that it's a matter of chance. But what I am coming to learn is that we are more than the sum of our experiences and nothing is a matter of chance. Rather, everything is a matter of choice. Something that took place over the course of a few seconds can have just as much influence on the story that I tell myself as an experience that transpired over an extended period of time—the tail ends up wagging the dog. I bought into a belief that my success, failures, careers, money in the bank defined my self-worth. They all are important players in my story, but they do not define who I am, what I am worth of or what I am capable of accomplishing. Past performance, good or bad, is not a guarantee of the future. It's time to turn the key and take ownership of my story. Not my parents', friends', family, kids', colleagues' stories, but my own. It won't be easy, but it will be worth it. Also, I am worthy. Worthy of reason. Worthy of love. Worthy of generosity. Worthy of accomplishing big things.

REFLECT

- How have I perceived myself?

- How would I like to see myself?

- How do I see others?

- What part of my story do I struggle to own? How do I stop myself from owning it?

- What false stories do I hold onto? How did I acquire them? Why have I held onto them?

- What true stories do I hold onto? How did I acquire them? Why have I held onto them?

RESPOND

- How will I respond to victory?

- How will I respond to disappointment?

- How do I clear a path for the future?

- Why will owning my story benefit me?

- What stories will I discard starting today?

- What stories will I embrace and carry forward starting today?

- Why is today the day I start to own my story?

Faith, Family, Fitness, Friends, Finances & Fun
CURRENT REALITY
- What is going well? Why?

- Why do I like it?

- What is not going well? Why is it not going well?

- How are my top beliefs of activities helping or hindering me?

DESIRED REALITY

- Why does my desired reality look better?

- Why will adopting new activities or beliefs help me?

- How will I approach developing new activities and beliefs?

Part 3
GIFTS

MEETING CHAZ

The lobby of the arena was a hive of activity. It was 4:45 p.m. on the nose, but there was no sign of The Janitor, so Steve stood in the back watching things unfold. People moved in and out of the lobby and theater spaces; they were carrying props, moving boxes and setting up merchandise booths. There was a sense of purpose behind each step, but the thing that stood out the most was the joy that permeated the room. It was apparent that everyone was fully engaged and present in what they were doing. Their movements almost seemed choreographed. That is, except for the large security guard making a beeline for Steve. His movements were just as purposeful, but they were not a part of the dance going on in the background.

"My apologies sir, we're glad you're excited to see the concert, but doors don't open for another 90 minutes."

Just as he was about to explain what he was doing there, Steve heard a voice from behind him, "Sorry guys! He's with me."

They both turned to see Chaz Cho walking toward them. Other than the fact she was wearing yoga pants and a hoodie, she looked exactly like the picture Steve had seen on the Janitor's wall.

"Thank you so much. He's a guest of mine," Chaz continued. "I'm expecting another guest as well. He's an older man—"

Before she could complete her sentence, a loud "Yoo Hoo!" rang out from the hallway. His waving at them might have clued them in, but both Chaz and Steve could tell it was The Janitor jogging down the hall toward the lobby.

"You're welcome, Ma'am," the security guard smiled. "Have a great performance tonight."

The Janitor caught up to Chaz and Steve just as the security guard was walking away. Chaz immediately embraced him. "It's been a while since I've had to jog like that," The Janitor said, catching his breath. "I got here a bit early and decided to go for a stroll around the arena to stretch my legs. Lost track of time."

"I'm beyond thrilled that you are here," Chaz said looking at The Janitor and Steve. "Let's head to my dressing room and catch up. We have about an hour before you'll have to head out to your seats. I've got you a couple in the VIP section."

"I like the sound of that. Pays to know people in high places, doesn't it?" The Janitor winked at Steve as they followed Chaz to her dressing room.

"Make yourself at home," Chaz said. "There is coffee, water and tea over there. I have some of my favorite snack foods on the table, but if you need anything let me know. I know they're not Angelica's, but I can have the kitchen whip up some PB & Js."

"Ha!" Steve laughed. "You know about the sand-wiches, too?"

"Of course! Anyone who's spent more than an hour with the man knows about his love for a good PB & J."

"That is very kind of you to offer, Chaz, but I am good for now." The Janitor said as sat down in a huge lounge chair. "We are grateful that you made some room for us in your schedule on such short notice."

"Anything for you," Chaz said with a smile.

The Janitor looked over at Steve and said, "I told her a little bit about how we met, but why don't you fill in the blanks."

"The long and short of it is the path I was on almost cost me everything, including my life. Now I'm trying to find the one I've always been meant to be on."

"Sounds like a worthy quest. How's it going so far?" Chaz inquired.

"I'm just getting started. One thing I know for sure is that it's a process that will require deep work and a willingness to let others help me along the way, which I've never been good at."

Steve thought about the times in his life when he ignored people's offers to help. "I've always been a stubborn 'DIY' guy, even when I was sure that the task I was doing wasn't in my wheelhouse and I had no business doing it."

The Janitor leaned forward in curiosity, "Like what, for example?"

"It's kind of a silly example but it's the first one that comes to mind because it was so embarrassing," Steve continued. "I put my kid's basketball hoop to-gether–backward."

"What do you mean backward?" The Janitor ribbed.

"So Santa Claus brought my girls one of those portable basketball hoops as a Christmas gift, but it needed to be assembled. I had a look at what was required and determined that I could do it myself despite the instructions explicitly indicating it was a two-person job."

"You are stubborn," Chaz said with a smirk.

"It gets better," Steve said. "I put out a table and laid out all the parts section by section. The first step was to connect the two pole sections. This was a no-fail mission. If I set them up incorrectly there was no turning back. I would be toast and so would the Christmas surprise, so I spent like ten minutes making sure I had things lined up properly."

"Oh no," cringed The Janitor.

"Nope, nope," Steve said with a smile. "I got it right! Or at least I thought I did until I read the next part of the instructions which told me I had to place a screw through a hole. Here's the thing. The hole did not exist."

"What do you mean it didn't exist?" asked Chaz.

"Well, at first I thought I screwed up the alignment and covered the hole. Like I said, it would have sunk the entire project. But then I reviewed the instructions and they said I had to drill a hole through the metal. Through the stinkin' metal! Who does that?" Steve sighed with laughter. "And the kicker is I didn't have the right kind of drill."

"So what did you do?" Chaz and The Janitor asked at the same time.

"Paid a visit to the neighborhood handyman, every neighborhood has one, and borrowed a drill, put in the hole and everyone lived happily ever after."

"Really?"

"Not exactly. Things went pretty smoothly from that point. I put the parts together section by section and was feeling super proud that I was doing the 'dad' thing and assembling this gift for my girls. And I had done a two-person job all by myself."

"And then?" asked The Janitor.

"And then my pride was shattered as I lifted up the basketball hoop.

"It was entirely backward?"

"Yes, and I didn't come to this discovery alone," Steve continued. "Remember the guy I borrowed the drill from? He was driving by and honked at me just as I was proudly raising the hoop. It was an intimate moment between two men. I walked over, handed him his drill along with my man card. Then he drove away never to be seen again."

"That's pretty bad," Chaz said biting her finger in a futile attempt not to laugh.

"Yup, it still stings," Steve chuckled sarcastically.

"What's a man card?" The Janitor asked.

"It's a card that lists out all the things a grown man allegedly must be able to do: use a tape measure, change a tire, smoke a brisket, oh, and assemble a basketball hoop."

"That's the most ridiculous thing I've ever heard of!" The Janitor said laughing.

"I am now acutely aware that my true gifts do not include most of the items listed on the man card.

Death had to knock some sense into me, but I am finally ready to ask for help." Steve paused and looked at The Janitor. "He has been so generous opening up his home and relationships to me, especially after I had written him off as just some second-class citizen taking out the trash."

"It's okay, Steve. I didn't think much of him either when we first met," Chaz joked.

THE AUDITION

Chaz grabbed a picture frame off the table and sat down across from The Janitor. "Did he tell you how we met?"

"Yeah. I can't imagine how painful that must have been for you."

"Birthdays are the most difficult time for me. My birthday, sure, but mostly theirs. This picture was taken at my sixteenth birthday party a few days before the accident. This is my dad," Chaz continued, pointing to the man in the picture. "He was the pillar of the family and my mom was the stereotypical tiger mom. He was so hard working, but he always talked to us about our God-given gifts and made room for us to dream. My mom was way more focused on the practical parts—the nuts and bolts of raising a couple of curious girls."

Steve thought about his own curious girls at home. "So who gave you the gift of music?"

"Both sides. Every family gathering included at least one jam session. My mom's parents played the piano and the fiddle. My dad's mom, the one I lived with after they passed, would sit in and sing along.

My sister and I would sit there mesmerized by the sounds they would create."

Steve got up and poured himself a cup of coffee. "Did you ever feel pressure to play?"

"Not at all. I felt a strong desire to play. I saw the joy it brought them, and their music made me feel happy. I was curious if I could do the same. I was drawn to the violin. Growing up, I thought the bow was a wand with magical powers and when I was nine I asked my parents if I could learn to play. They never locked me in a practice room or even insisted I practice for any length of time. Instead, it was daily and deeply intentional practice. Zero aimless effort. Even if it were for only five minutes, it had to be consistent and perfect practice. I ended up getting really good, and then I quit after they died."

"I figured that playing would have been an emotional outlet or something," Steve said timidly.

"I couldn't even if I wanted to, which I didn't. My violin broke the same day my heart did."

"How did your violin break?"

"I qualified to audition for a children's orchestra in Philadelphia," Chaz said as she grabbed a handful of popcorn from the bowl on the coffee table. "Getting a spot would open doors to some of the most prestigious music schools in the world. My parents decided to fly my grandma and me out a few days early so I could get rid of some of the performance jitters. My parents and my sister decided to make a road trip out of it. My dad called me a couple days before the audition to say they were on their way despite some terrible weather. That night a portion of the road they were on had washed out and they went right into it. They were killed instantly."

Steve handed Chaz a box of tissues. "So sorry. How did you find out?"

"The morning of the audition came and we still had not heard from them. My grandma was getting concerned," Chaz said wiping tears from her eyes. "She went down to the hotel lobby to call my parents. I was so focused on the audition that I tuned out the possibility that something was wrong. So I just kept visualizing my performance and going through my warm-up routine when I heard some commotion outside the door.

Someone was weeping and it sounded like my grandma. I walked over to the door, still holding my violin and looked through the peephole. Apparently, my grandma overheard a police officer asking for us when she went down to the lobby. I opened the door and asked what was going on. My grandma looked at me and started to weep uncontrollably into the officer's chest.

Deep inside I knew they were gone, but then she took a deep breath, turned toward me and said eight words that are forever burned into my memory—there was a car accident and they died—the next thing I remember is waking up on the floor, with what was left of my violin pinned underneath me."

Chaz stood up and walked over to pour herself some water. "My world shattered that day and my sense of self and security went with it. When I came to live with my grandma, I was very scattered."

"No offense, Chaz, but you were more than scattered," The Janitor added.

"You're right," laughed Chaz. "You know those old pinball machines with the ball and the levers? Well, I was an angry pinball, wreaking havoc everywhere I went. My grandma lived closest to where I grew up, so I moved in with her and finished high school. It was rough. I didn't fit in with anyone. I was a loner and didn't feel connected to anything. I just wanted to be like other girls my age: a mom to help me get ready for prom, a dad to joke with about my awkward date and a sister to share boy stories with. To make matters worse, I went through a goth phase. It was brief, but it was bad."

"Is that what it's called? I always wondered," The Janitor smiled. "I'll never forget the first time your grandma brought you to the office."

"Neither will I," Chaz laughed.

The Janitor stood up and began to re-enact his first impression of Chaz. "Let me paint the picture for you, Steve. I wanted to create a happy environment in our offices, so we always kept our offices brightly lit and our walls were painted with what I called happy colors. So one day, I am walking into the office and Chaz's grandma is coming at me with a very serious look on her face. She started to apologize for bringing Chaz to work. I told her not to worry. No big deal. And then I saw her standing next to the shredding machine. In this sea of bright light and happy colors was a sullen girl wearing black and gray clothes, military boots with spikes on them, black lipstick and jet black hair. I mean, I think even the headphones you were wearing were black."

"Yup, they were. I think I still have them somewhere."

"As I walked toward you, you looked at me and pulled off your headphones. You had the same concerned looked as your grandma. Anyway, I put my hand out to shake yours and said, 'I'm so glad you're here.'"

"To which I responded, 'Whatever' and put my headphones back on," Chaz said shaking her head in embarrassment. "And that was the beginning of what would become a beautiful friendship."

"Beautiful is right."

"The truth is I didn't know how to respond," Chaz said looking at Steve. "He may have been the first person to introduce himself without apologizing for the loss of my family. Little by little all the bright lights and happy colors in that place began to rub off on me and my wardrobe."

"And you started to play again?" asked Steve.

"That came later. I let my walls down enough to go see a therapist and talk through some of my issues, but I still didn't feel like playing. Besides, I didn't have a violin."

"Right, I forgot."

"Anyway, at the end of one of our sessions, the therapist asked me if I might be interested in being a counselor at a summer camp for kids who had lost a parent. The camp was located upstate and sat on a gorgeous lake surrounded by trees that we referred to as The Sentinels. It was wonderful. I felt like

I finally fit in someplace. One of my favorite parts of the camp was the weekly talent show put on by the campers. It was mostly silly skits, jokes or magic tricks, but it was a time where everyone let loose. Lots of laughter and full of joy.

"What I didn't realize until the last week of camp was the camp had a tradition of having two talent shows: one put on by the kids and one put on by the adults and the counselors. And everyone was expected to participate. I hadn't performed anything, even a silly skit, since my family died. I panicked and called my grandma. She assured me that she would be there to support me and that whatever I did would be great."

"So what happened?"

"Something incredible, that's what!" The Janitor interrupted before Chaz could respond.

"You were there, too?" Steve asked.

"Several of us went to the talent show with her grandma for moral support."

"So the day of the talent show came and I still didn't know what to do. I figured maybe I could tell some jokes. I grabbed a joke book from the camp library and walked down to the lake to practice. That's when I heard it. One of the kids had brought a violin and was practicing *Twinkle, Twinkle Little Star.*"

"Fortuitous," Steve interjected.

"Very. My hands started to sweat, but I knew exactly what I was supposed to do. I needed to ask that kid if I could borrow it for the counselor talent show. He reluctantly agreed, but not without first warning me about how difficult it was to learn how to play an instrument like the violin. I told him I appreciated the warning and ran to call my grandma, but then decided I would surprise her instead.

"I remember walking up to the stage and repeating this quote I had heard *Music is life. Music is Peace. Music is Hope.* I looked out at the audience. Staring back at me were kids and counselors who had lost everything. I explained that tonight would be the first time I had played any music since losing my family. And I would be playing *Meditation*, the piece I was supposed to audition with. I turned to look at my grandma. She was covering her mouth, but I could tell by the crease in her eyes that she was smiling. I smiled back, took a deep breath, rested the violin on my shoulder and began to play. I could feel my family and friends leaning in as I moved from note to note.

"When I finished, I burst into tears. I looked out and the audience was clapping and shouting 'thank you' over and over. At that moment, I recognized music was simply an expression of my true gift."

"So what's your actual gift then?"

"To help people heal. To help them feel understood. To help them feel joy, hope and connected. Music was simply the most natural way for me to express that gift. And since music is something practically everyone could relate to in some fashion, I decided to pursue it as my life's mission. To this day, I still consider that silly talent show as the most important audition of my life."

Rediscover Gifts

Steve closed his eyes and took a deep, intentional breath as a familiar sensation welled up in him. He began to feel sorry for himself, even angry. After all, he didn't have a clue how to begin looking for his gifts and the thought of how much time it might take to develop them was daunting.

"What about the rest of us normal folks?" Steve asked sarcastically.

"What do you mean?" Chaz responded.

"Well, I would imagine that most people are as clueless as I am."

Steve noticed a stack of souvenir coffee mugs on a table across the room walked over, grabbed one and sat back down. Then he pulled some pens out of his pocket and placed them in the mug.

"The only thing I know for sure is that most of the time I feel like this souvenir coffee mug with pens in it. I'm doing something, but not necessarily the right thing."

"So you're a frustrated coffee mug?" Chaz joked.

"Sounds funny, I know. But yeah, kinda. It's exactly how I feel right now. I don't have any idea what my gifts are, and I seriously doubt that I have any that are worthy of being performed on stage."

"Steve," The Janitor began. "I can relate to the feeling of being that coffee mug with pens in it, but we all have gifts. It's a sacred promise. No matter what you do, your gifts can never be taken from you. Perhaps this is another cave you need to enter. You may need to find your way back to the deepest, darkest part of the cave to unearth your gift or gifts. And as Shakespeare said, *the whole world's a stage!* So when you emerge, you will be ready, willing and able to share what you've found on any stage required of you—big or small."

"May I challenge your thinking, Steve?" Chaz asked reaching for the coffee mug.

"Please."

"What is the purpose of a coffee mug or any cup for that matter?"

"To carry a hot or cold beverage to my mouth."

"Expressed in its ideal form that is true. But isn't the core purpose of a cup to simply carry something: coffee, tea, whiskey, pens, paper clips, etc.? Why not pens?"

"I suppose so."

"The reality is that from time to time, we may not be able to express our gift in the ideal way, but it doesn't mean it's not there or any less valuable. Think about it this way. If they took away my violin, would they be taking away my gift? No! Don't get me wrong," Chaz continued. "It would suck, but I'd find another way to express it. And the case of this coffee mug, it is still carrying something, just not the ideal thing."

"I see your point, but it is still a hard pill to swallow. The reason I feel like a frustrated coffee mug is because it feels like someone put the pens in without asking my permission."

"Ah ha," said Chaz. "There lies the rub."

"The truth is I've become addicted to pleasing other people. I like people and I enjoy being liked by those people. So I end up doing things or taking on projects and tasks that feel completely unnatural and quite often suck the life out of me. It totally backfires on me, too, because I get bitter, they get resentful and I end up back on square one—alone."

"Hot dog!" The Janitor said clapping his hands together. "The journey can feel lonely at times, but I assure it is not just a solitary process. I can't wait for you to meet Fidel tomorrow. He has a very powerful question he uses to deal with the issue of living out other people's stories."

"And you're going to leave me in suspense until then?"

The Janitor provided a mischievous smirk as his answer.

"Don't worry, Steve," Chaz said. "He does this to everyone he likes. And you're going to love Fidel. Wait until you see his library. It's truly something to behold!"

Steve made a mental note to bring a copy of a book Fidel might enjoy adding to his collection.

"In the meantime," Chaz continued, "let me share some tips that The Janitor gave me and that proved to be very helpful in my journey to rediscover my gifts and put them to work."

"I'm all ears."

"After I finished Julliard, I became obsessed with playing on the biggest stages because it would boost my status, not to mention my wallet. I became so obsessed that every other area of my life suffered, especially my health. My grandma invited him over to speak some sense into me. Do you remember what you said?" Chaz asked looking at The Janitor.

"Free yourself from the pursuit of status and watch what you create. Focus on how you nurture your gifts because it influences the way you engage in the world and affects the role you play in other people's stories."

"That night I recommitted to the pursuit of music as the primary way to express my gift to connect, heal and bring joy into the lives of others. I asked myself: what would be the best way for *me* to serve others? My mind exploded with creative ideas, but there was one that just kept popping up repeatedly. I decided to be a soloist and create a hybrid of classical music with modern-day pop. I didn't know how it would all work but I embarked on this journey with the intent to give it away unconditionally, no strings attached with an understanding that I might never witness the impact my gift has in the world."

"What do you mean?"

"I had to believe so strongly in sharing my gifts with others that I would do it even if it meant my work would not be heard until I was dead and gone."

The Janitor got up and walked over to the platters of food on the table and started munching. "You know," The Janitor said while popping grapes into his mouth, "I think one of my favorite attributes of any human being is humility. At the end of the day, it is the fertile ground from which our gifts will grow. And if you seed it with a dash of curiosity and a pinch of wonder, you will be off to a good start but where people mess up most is in their relationship with time."

"You mean time management?" Steve asked.

"No. I mean time tolerance. People just don't have patience. They want things now and when they don't see immediate results they quit. Reminds me of an experience I had in India. Have I ever told you about that trip?"

Both Chaz and Steve shook their heads.

"I was in India consulting with a company in Kolkata. At the end of the engagement, the group asked me if I would like to see the living bridges of Meghalaya. Always up for an adventure, I said yes and the next day, after a quick flight and a few bus rides, we arrived at our destination."

"What did they look like?" Steve asked.

"It was something straight out of Indiana Jones," The Janitor continued. "The locals didn't know exactly when their ancestors started building these living root bridges but they are constructed using the aerial roots of the rubber trees located along the river. The locals will guide the roots from one side to another, use rocks and bamboo as scaffolding and allow the bridge to strengthen until it is strong enough to bear the weight of a human."

"Sounds remarkable," Chaz marveled.

"But the thing that blew my mind is the fact they can take up to 15 years to complete and a well-built root bridge can last for hundreds of years. In fact, the one they showed me was estimated to be 500 years old."

"Now that takes time tolerance!" Steve laughed.

Chaz stood up from her chair. "Speaking of time, I need to begin preparing for tonight's show."

"Thank you so much for sharing your story with me," Steve said reaching out to shake Chaz's hand. "You've given me a lot to think about. And I can't wait to see you in action!"

"You're very welcome, Steve! You're in good hands with this guy right here," Chaz said putting her arm around The Janitor's neck. "One final thought: when you come out of that cave with your gift in hand, you may feel uncomfortable using it at first. Whatever you do, don't give up. One day, the practice and effort will pay off and you will more than know it; you will feel it. Your gift will produce an experience that takes people on a journey from one place to the next. From where they are now to just a little bit closer to where they desire to be."

"I would like that," Steve said. "I don't know exactly how or what that means yet, but I want that feeling."

"Well," The Janitor said. "You're well on your way. Speaking of being on your way, we will be on ours and head over to the VIP lounge. See you for dinner on Sunday night, Chaz?"

"Wouldn't miss it! Oh and I had them put something special in the lounge for you guys."

"PB & Js?"

"You got it."

"You're too kind, Chaz." The Janitor smiled as they walked out the door and into the hall. "Too kind."

"So what do you think?" The Janitor asked Steve as they walked to the lounge.

"About Chaz? She great. Can't wait to see her perform."

"Yeah, Chaz is incredible. But what do you think about your gifts?"

"To be honest, I don't know. I'm still processing everything that's happened in the last few days. And right now, I feel like I'm drinking from a firehose."

"Well, keep it up. You're moving in the right direction. Still up for meeting Fidel tomorrow?"

"I think so. I don't want to lose the momentum."

As they took their seats, PB & Js in hand, Steve looked around at all the people in the audience. They were hungry to feel the joy and healing that Chaz promised to deliver. At the same time, however, Steve battled with old voices in his head saying he didn't have any gifts and he wasn't born for anything. But for the moment, he decided to shut them away and simply allow himself to be moved, directed and healed by her music. And moved he was. As soon as the curtains rose and Chaz hit the first note, his heart and mind were full of joy. Not just because of the amazing music, but because he was witnessing someone give away their gift in the most stunning way. The years of effort and practice, combined with

an intimate knowledge of her gift enabled her to play
with a deep, rich emotion. It was clear she was creating something special, something unforgettable.

Steve took out his phone to text Lucy.

> Hey babe -

> Wish you were here.

> This concert is something special.

> Want to create something unforgettable with me?

Was just thinking about you.

It's been so weird not having you here...

We MISS YOU!!!

And of course I want to create something unforgettable.

> Awesome :-)

Can't wait to meet everyone on Sunday.

I'll be asleep when you get home.

Don't forget to kiss me when you go to bed.

Why? Lol.

Because I need one.

I may be asleep, but I'm not dead ;-)

THE AFFIRMATION

The house may have been quiet when Steve returned home from the concert but his heart and mind were far from quiet. His thoughts were galloping away within the confines of his mind! Everyone was asleep just as Lucy had predicted, so he decided to take advantage of the stillness and reflect on what his gifts were and how he might use them.

He sat at the dining room table, took out his journal and attempted to write, but nothing came to him. The empty page stared back at him. It was as if the page were taunting him and saying "you don't have any gifts." Steve slammed the journal shut. He crossed his arms, leaned back from the table and let out a deep, frustrated sigh; then he decided to open the journal and give it another shot. Nothing.

His hand began to quiver with emotion as he reflected on all that had transpired over the last few months. He rested his face into his folded arms on the table and began to cry quietly.

Lucy came out of their room wrapped in her bathrobe and stood quietly looking at Steve. A man who, prior to the heart attack, had morphed into a formidable mountain. A mountain she was uncertain she'd ever been able to approach, let alone summit. And now, here was her man, the man she fell in love with, weeping at the table. He was still a mountain, but one made low.

"Are you okay?" Lucy asked gently placing her hand on Steve's shoulder.

"No, not really!" Steve said without lifting his head to look at Lucy. "I should be feeling great, but I don't. Physically, I'm the best I've felt in ages. Our marriage is moving in the right direction. And my relationship with the girls is phenomenal." Steve paused for a moment. "But I feel so mediocre. I don't know, I guess I'm afraid."

"Of what?" Lucy asked sitting by his side.

"A ton of stuff. Of letting you and the girls down again," Steve continued. "Of doing work that feels useless or doesn't matter. I spent all this time with The Janitor and Chaz today talking about gifts and decided to do some journaling but look at this page. It's empty. At best I'm confused about what my gifts are. But, if I'm being really honest, I just don't know if I have any at all."

"Do you really believe that?" Lucy asked incredulously.

"I don't know what to believe."

"Babe, look at me," Lucy continued, placing her hands on his face. "Let me try to put your heart to rest a little. I commit to you that I will never give up on you. No matter what. Do you believe me?"

"Yes."

"Say it."

"I believe that you will never give up on me."

"There will be days for both of us when it won't be easy but we can survive anything as long as we're together."

Steve let out a big sigh.

"You've always had the most transparent sighs, hon," Lucy giggled. "The question about your gifts is really bothering you, isn't it?"

"It is. Think I have any?"

"Well, I've always said you have the gift of gab," Lucy joked trying to add some levity to the conversation.

"True," Steve laughed.

"All kidding aside, you are one of the most gifted people I know. You have this uncanny ability to connect with people and build relationships almost instantaneously. But I think your greatest gift is insight. It's how you won me over, anyway."

"I thought it was my charm and stunning good looks."

"It was your insight first, second and third. Your charm and stunning good looks came in fourth and fifth," Lucy winked. "Seriously though, remember when we were engaged and I was stressing about taking the job at that marketing agency? I liked everything about the company: the people, the place, the salary and benefits. It was really the perfect job for me, so perfect that my parents could not understand why it was taking me so long to accept the offer. I couldn't figure out why I was so conflicted. We went out for a hike and you asked me a potentially nuclear question."

"I asked if you thought you were conflicted because you wanted to be a stay-at-home mom."

"That was it! Stopped me in my tracks, literally and figuratively."

"I was scared to death to ask that question."

"As you should have been," Lucy laughed. "We weren't even married yet. My parents were pissed when I didn't take the job, but your insight was spot on and I was absolutely clear on what I wanted. It wouldn't have been right for me to take the job knowing my heart and mind would not be all in."

"You think those are gifts?"

"Absolutely! Powerful ones. I'm sure they both played a role in your early success before..." Lucy hesitated.

"Things got off track?"

"Yes."

"What if I don't want to continue doing what I've been doing?"

Lucy paused and thought for a moment. "You know, I don't have an answer to that, but it is something I am completely open to discussing. You know me, uncertainty makes me uncomfortable, but I am confident of this: I am with you and for you. Those gifts are transferable to nearly any industry or career and if you work on developing and mastering them you will be unstoppable. Just never stop talking and sharing with me, okay?"

"Okay. And thank you."

"For what?"

"For believing in me, in us, when I couldn't."

"When I say yes, it actually means something. Now come to bed. That journal can wait until the morning, but I can't. I still need that kiss I asked for."

REFLECT AND RESPOND

THOUGHTS FROM STEVE'S JOURNAL

First, owning my story and now my gifts. It is
clear that I need to think differently about
gifts. I've always looked at gifts as something
that could help me earn a position or some kind
of outcome. And when it didn't come to
fruition, I would revert back to old stories of
not being good or worthy. It's no wonder that I
have been so frustrated by my lack of clarity
around my gifts. Gifts are not meant to give me
status. They exist to lift others up or help them
along their journey. I need to free myself from
the notion that my gifts translate to a higher
status. Doing so will take discipline, but as The
Janitor said humility is the fertile soil from
which my gifts will grow. It's bigger than playing an
instrument or writing a poem or designing a plan
for someone. After all, if those expressions are
taken away and it's all gone, what would I have
left? The real gifts are the intention behind
the expression. How I explore and develop my
gifts will significantly influence the way I show up
in the world and will affect the role that I play
in other people's stories. Each and every
encounter is an opportunity for me to facilitate
my purpose. It may not be the perfect expression
of my purpose and that is okay.

REFLECTION

- What brings me joy?

- Have I brought others joy? How?

- Why is having gifts and using them important to me?

- Why do I allow obstacles to get in the way and prevent me from fully expressing my gifts?

- What clues about my gifts may be hidden in my current level of knowledge and abilities?

- How have I attached my self-worth to my gifts?

RESPOND

- How will I approach taking inventory of my gifts? Why is this important?

- How will I prevent fear from dictating what skills and gifts I am capable of developing?

- What kind of effort am I willing to put into uncovering and developing my gifts? How will habits help me?

- How will developing time tolerance help me?

- What can I create right now?

- How will I acknowledge the gifts others give or share with me?

Part 4
ACTION

Meeting Fidel

"Daddy!" Tina and Elle shouted as they jumped onto the bed, waking Steve up from a deep slumber. He grabbed them both, wrapped them up in his arms and squeezed them close to his chest.

"Can you hear it?" Steve whispered.

"Hear what, Daddy?" Tina whispered back.

"The engine of my heart beating with so much love for the two of you." Steve roared with laughter as he tickled his two daughters.

"You're so silly, Daddy," Elle giggled. "Your heart's not an engine. It's a heart."

"You are so right, munchkin. You have no idea just how right you are." And with that, the girls jumped off the bed and went dancing out of the room.

Steve stood up and caught his reflection in the mirror. He looked refreshed. He felt refreshed. But as he was getting ready to meet Fidel, those dang butterflies showed up in his stomach again. This time Steve decided they were there because he was doing something that took him outside his comfort zone. After all, Fidel was one of the most successful businessmen in the city and despite feeling physically and emotionally rejuvenated, Steve felt like he was an utter business disaster.

Just as he was walking out the door, his phone buzzed with a text message:

> It's Fidel. Can you meet me at City High's track and field arena?

> I'm going for a run.

> Mind if I drive back to my office in your car?

The thought of picking up Fidel made Steve even more nervous.

> Sure. My car's a little messy.

> Wasn't planning on chauffeuring anyone today. lol.

> Ha. No worries.

> My car is always in a state of chaos.

> See you soon.

After a quick pit stop at a drive-through car wash, Steve's car was now in an acceptable state for guests.

He pulled into the track parking lot, walked into the arena and sat down in the stands.

Fidel was the only person on the track. He may have been in his fifties, but he looked as young as, or younger than, Steve. In addition to being a successful businessman, Steve discovered Fidel was also a competitive long-distance runner and held quite a few records in the sport.

Steve wasn't a runner himself, but at the moment it seemed like Fidel was sprinting more than running. He came blazing around the turn of the track and sprinted straight through an invisible finish line. It appeared as if he checked the stopwatch on his wrist and then threw his hands up in victory. He turned and walked toward the edge of the track and started waving.

"That you, Steve?"

"In the flesh," Steve said, kicking himself for the cheesy response.

"Give me 10 minutes to clean up and I'll meet you in the parking lot."

"Sounds good."

Steve was waiting outside the locker rooms when Fidel tapped the passenger side window and waved at Steve with a gigantic grin.

Even the guy's teeth are perfect, Steve thought quietly.

"Hey, thanks for being flexible and meeting here."

"Not a problem," Steve said, reaching out to shake Fidel's hand. "Thank you for taking the time. It's nice to finally meet you in person."

"Let's head to my office. Know where it is?"

Steve knew Fidel's office was in the same building as The Janitor's company and Outlier Capital. "Actually, I used to work at Outlier Capital. It's in the same building."

"Small world," Fidel said looking at his phone. "I have a ton of messages that I need to reply to. Mind if I take care of that right now?"

"Go for it."

A few minutes later, Fidel put his phone back in his pocket, closed his eyes and reclined back in the seat. Steve didn't know exactly what to say, but the silence was making him incredibly anxious.

"So," Steve began as his brain searched for a relevant question to break the silence. "Are you training for something?"

"Always," Fidel said. "I don't have any major events coming up, but I want to be ready to go if an opportunity presents itself."

"Been competing long?"

Fidel rolled down the window and put his arm out. "Do you mind? Need some fresh air."

"No, not at all," Steve said rolling his window down as well.

"I started running in high school and fell in love with the sport."

"I find it amazing when people say they love running," Steve laughed. "I've hated it ever since I was a little kid."

"Why?"

"Well, I just always felt like I was going to run out of air."

Fidel rolled up the window and turned toward Steve. "Getting a good breathing rhythm is important. With a little coaching, I'm sure you'd get comfortable with it."

"Maybe," Steve said while in the back of his mind he was thinking *not a chance.*

"I ended up running in college, too," Fidel continued. "Contemplated trying out for the Olympic team but one thing lead to another and it didn't work out."

Steve was curious to hear what prevented Fidel from trying out for the Olympics but didn't want to come off as being nosy, so he didn't pry.

"Now I run mostly for the fun of it."

As Steve exited the highway and turned into the parking garage, he heard a familiar electronic beep. For most, it was a mundane sound that went unnoticed, but not for Steve. It was a sound that reminded him of what had nearly happened a few months earlier. For a brief moment, he was haunted by the thought of repeating past mistakes.

"You okay?" Fidel asked.

"Me? Yeah, I'm good."

"My mom used to say *there's a thousand songs sung in a sigh.*"

"Didn't realize I sighed."

"Which ones are you singing?"

"Don't know. Not much of a singer," Steve said in an attempt to make light of the way he was feeling.

"You can park in my spot near the elevator bank."

"Great," Steve said pulling into the parking spot. Before getting out, he reached into the back and grabbed a bag from the back seat and then followed Fidel to the elevators.

The elevator doors opened right into Fidel's office, just like The Janitor's. Steve couldn't believe it. As he scanned the office, he wasn't sure if he had stepped into a library or a place of business. Polished bookshelves wrapped around nearly the entire space. The shelves were stacked with books, and each section had one of those rolling ladders to move from side to side. Steve had never seen anything like it in person. The view from the windows wasn't bad either. Looking out to the city below was an ornate, mahogany desk with a phone, a laptop, a few books, and floating a few feet above it was a loft with some lounge chairs, bean bags, and a fire pole that descended to the area just behind the desk.

"Wait, I've got to show you something."

Fidel went up the stairs to the loft.

"Welcome to my office!" Fidel laughed as he slid down a fire pole that descended to the area just behind his desk.

"This place is something else. I don't know if I've ever seen so many books outside the city library and I've definitely never been in an office with a fire pole."

"Isn't it cool! I took a page from The Janitor's lookbook when I designed my office. For him it's pictures of his friends, for me it's books. Check this out."

Fidel placed his hand on Steve's elbow and guided him toward one of the bookshelves. "This office space is really too big for me, but I needed a space large enough for my book collection."

"Why not your home?"

"I travel a lot for work, so I only keep a modest apartment in the city."

"This side of the room is full of books that I've read at least once. And that side is full books I intend to read. And over there," Fidel continued, pointing to his desk, "I have four books that I refer to on a regular basis, sometimes daily."

"And what are they?"

"The Bible. I didn't have one growing up in Cuba, but when I arrived here a nice couple gave me one. It's become a remarkable resource for my spiritual and personal growth. The next one is a book called *Aspire: Discover Your Life's Purpose Through the Power of Words* by Kevin Hall. That one introduced me to another incredible book called *Man's Search for Meaning* by Viktor Frankl. Then my sister gifted me a copy of a book called *Visioneering* by Andy Stanley. That one has been a game changer for me, too."

Steve made a mental note about adding those books to his own reading list.

"Well, speaking of gifts," Steve said reaching into his bag. "In the off chance you don't already own a copy, I have a book to add to your collection."

Steve handed Fidel the hundredth-anniversary edition of *Endurance: Shackleton's Incredible Voyage* by Alfred Lansing.

"Wow. Thank you, Steve. Very kind of you."

"You're welcome."

"Make yourself comfortable," Fidel said guiding Steve to a set of well-used leather chairs and a transparent coffee table in the middle of the room. "The

Janitor should be here shortly, but may I get you anything to drink in the meantime?"

"Coffee would be great."

Fidel poured himself and Steve a fresh cup of coffee and then joined Steve on one of the lounge chairs. "I've read this book many times but, believe it or not, I don't actually own a copy. It's an incredible story!

Just then, the phone on Fidel's desk began to ring and he hurried over to pick it up.

"This is Fidel."

"Oh hey," Fidel said with a smile and looked at Steve. "Are you on the way down from your office? Yup, he's right here. It's The Janitor. He wants to talk to you."

"Steve," The Janitor said. "So sorry, but I can't make it today. I'm working on a couple things and just can't get away but I wanted to check with you on something."

"No problem. What's up?"

"I'm planning a surprise for Sunday night and I just wanted to make sure you'd be okay with that."

"For me?"

"Yes, for you."

"That's kind of you, but you don't need..."

"I know I don't need to, but if you're good with surprises, I'd like to. That okay with you?" The Janitor interrupted.

"Um, sure. Yes. Why not?"

"It's going to be special, I promise. Oh and one more thing."

"Yeah?"

"Have you ever seen so many books?"

Steve started to laugh, "No. It's insane."

"Give Fidel my best. See you guys tomorrow evening."

"Will do."

Steve hung up the phone and walked back to the comfy chairs and his cup of coffee.

"Not able to make it?" Fidel asked.

"Said he's working on a couple projects. He also asked if I was okay with surprises. Is that weird?"

"That guy's always got something up his sleeve."

Fidel picked up his coffee mug and walked over to refill it. "You good?"

"I'll take a little warm up," Steve said handing his mug to Fidel.

"We can talk about books all day, but I don't believe that is why you're here."

"No. Not really," Steve said as he sat on the couch and picked up his coffee mug. "But at the same time, I don't really know why I'm here."

"You mean like here in my office or more like 'what's the meaning of my life' here?" Fidel asked using air quotes.

Steve laughed. "Can it be both?"

"Earlier you said you used to work at Outlier. Have you left?"

"No. I am just unsure about what I should do."

"So you're feeling stranded."

"The conversations I've had with The Janitor and Chaz have been incredibly insightful, but I'm trying to figure out my next steps. I've lost a great deal of confidence in the last few years. Now I am constantly second-guessing myself."

Fidel could sense how desperately Steve wanted clarity. "What's the outcome that you want from these conversations?"

Steve tilted his head and reflected on the question as he sipped his coffee. "I want to rebuild my confidence, to learn how to trust myself again. But right now I'm frozen."

"Listen," Fidel continued with a sigh. "I know it's not ideal but none of us—not me, not Chaz, not even The Janitor—is in possession of the exact answer you're looking for. All we can do is share from our own experience and allow the truth that you possess inside you to resurface and show the way, or at least part of it."

"We all would love for the answers to be delivered on a magical silver platter," Steve said, "but yes, I've come to understand that isn't realistic."

Fidel paused and thumbed through the pages of the book until he got to a section with some of the black and white photos of Shackleton and his crew.

SETTING SAIL

"You know," Fidel continued. "I've felt like Shackleton many times in my life."

"How so?"

"Well, you have this grand plan built around realizing a dream that many have said was impossible. You get people to rally around and support you. You build a great team, go all in financially. Everything seems like it's going according to plan. Then, just as you're about to reach your goal, you get stuck and your plans get crushed.

There's no one there to champion your pursuit so your support dries up. Finances dwindle down to nothing. No one has a clue of what to do next or how to get back to where you started. With the dream dead and gone, you're left with two feelings: a mix of bewilderment and responsibility."

"Bewilderment and responsibility. Now that is something I can relate to!"

"But the idea of just giving up wasn't acceptable for Shackleton, and it's not an acceptable option for me, and it doesn't have to be for you."

Fidel got up from the couch and walked toward one of the bookshelves. "Come over here. I want to show you something. The problem isn't with feeling lost or even being lost. Both of those are okay," Fidel continued. "But where most of us screw up is when we decide to stay lost."

"I certainly don't want to stay lost."

Fidel grabbed something off the bookshelves and handed it to Steve.

"My mom and dad worked hard, but we were pretty poor, even by communist standards," Fidel stated matter of factly. "The one thing they always made sure of was that they had money for education. My dad emphasized that a good education would be our ticket to a better life."

Fidel pointed to the item in Steve's hand.

"Do you know what that is?"

Steve looked at the contraption in his hands. "A Bunsen burner? I haven't seen one of these things since nearly failing high school chemistry."

Fidel smiled.

"I had two dreams growing up: compete in the Olympics and become a doctor. Both were achievable and either one was a ticket to a better life."

"So what stopped you?" Steve asked recalling Fidel's earlier comment.

"My dad died the first week of my freshman year of college."

Steve was stunned. "I'm so sorry."

The phone on Fidel's desk began to ring again.

"Need to get that?"

"No. It can wait."

Steve caught Fidel wiping away a tear. "At the time, my mom was ill and my dad was the only one working," Fidel continued. "I had to drop out to support my mother and sister. I was devastated, not only for the loss of my father, but also because I had to let go of everything I had hoped and worked for."

Steve looked at the Bunsen burner again. "I don't mean to sound insensitive, but what does this have to do with your dad passing?"

"I was about to light that burner during a Chemistry lab when my professor pulled me out to tell me I had a family emergency and without even thinking I ran out of the lab with it. So now it's a reminder."

"Of what?" Steve asked.

"That no matter how bewildering it may seem, sometimes the original dream has to die for the real adventure to begin. Just like Shackleton."

Steve wondered for a moment about his own dreams as he handed the burner to Fidel and sat back down in the chair. It had been so long since he allowed himself to dream, let alone think about the opportunities that arose as a result of dreams unraveling.

"I left school and took over my dad's job as a cab driver," Fidel continued. "It was so depressing, but I had to support my mom and sister. At the time, that seemed like the most logical way to do it. One day I woke up and I couldn't get out of bed. A doctor friend of ours come over. I confided in him and shared how I had been feeling. Before he left he gave me a pivotal piece of advice: remember that whether you're alive or dead doesn't matter. What matters is what you live for and what you are prepared to die for. I knew I wasn't prepared to die as a taxi cab driver. That was the moment I decided to leave Cuba. Two years later I had saved up enough money and courage to do just that."

Steve was surprised that it took Fidel so long to leave. "Two years?"

"I couldn't just abandon my family. And I had to save up enough money to buy a spot on a boat and make sure I wasn't completely broke when I got here."

Steve was looking around the room when he spotted a globe of the earth in the corner of Fidel's office.

"How long did it take you to get to Miami?" Steve said walking over to the globe.

Fidel gave Steve a stern look. "Who said I went to Miami?"

Embarrassed by his assumption, Steve began to blush. "I mean, I just assumed that you would have landed there. At least that's what they show on the news."

"I kid, I kid," Fidel laughed. "I did end up in Miami, but it took me over a month to get there."

Steve searched the globe for Cuba. "Over a month? I figured it would be a day or two at most."

"It would have been if I left from Havana, but we sailed from the west coast of Cuba and ended up in Cancun," Fidel said using his finger to draw a line from Cuba to Mexico.

"Sailed, as on a sailboat?"

"No, actually. Forty of us were crammed below the deck of a fishing boat."

"Smelly."

"To say the least. This thing probably had a maximum capacity of twenty people. What made it even more cramped were the dozen 100-gallon barrels of oil. They stacked us in there like sardines and gave us each one bag of Cheetos and two liters of Gatorade. That was it.

In addition to us and the crew, there were two armed men. Not sure why they were there, but they definitely added to the fear. It took four days to get to the coast of Mexico and we had to stay below deck the entire trip. Eat, drink, go to the bathroom, all below deck. No light, nothing for four days. It was almost unbearable, but I kept reminding myself what was on the other side."

"Sounds—"

"Horrible?" Fidel interrupted. "Yes, but something all of us were willing to suffer for and would probably do again in a heartbeat."

"So you landed and the guys with guns guided you to the border?"

"I wish," Fidel said pulling up his sleeves to reveal leftover scar tissue on both arms.

"Ouch!"

"We were about a mile away from the coast when one of the barrels caught on fire. To this day, I am still not sure how it happened. But the smoke immediately filled up the space below deck and snuffed out any light that had crept in from above deck. Not only were we blind, but we also couldn't breathe, and the hatch could only be opened from above deck. We were screaming for our lives. All forty of us. It was so loud. A sound I will never forget.

One of the armed men heard the commotion and threw open the hatch. The dense, black smoke escaped first, followed by those of us below deck but not before myself and a few others were burned. The deck of the ship was chaos. The captain and crew were no were to be found, and neither were the armed guys. They had abandoned us. I remember looking at the huge plume of black smoke billowing into the sky when I heard some people yelling for us to jump in the water. Without thinking, I, along with everyone else on the boat, did just that. Fortunately, we were right off the coast of Cancun, one of the most popular tourist destinations in the world.

"That must have been surreal."

"It was weird. People had seen the smoke and came to the rescue. Unfortunately, the way it all went down, temporarily scuttled our attempt to take refuge in the US."

Steve was completely captivated by Fidel's story and was now even more impressed by all that Fidel had accomplished. "I would imagine so," Steve remarked. "Did they take you to the hospital or something?"

"When we arrived on shore, the Mexican police were waiting for us. Those of us with burns were taken to a local hospital for treatment and then transported to a holding facility in Mexico City. We were there for 30 days while they confirmed our Cuban citizenship. Once that was done, they released us and gave us two choices: stay in Mexico or find a way into the United States.

Miraculously, some Catholic missionaries heard about what happened and were waiting to take us in when we were released. I ended up staying with a couple named Marco and Juanita. In fact, they gave me the Bible that's on my desk. I told them what I wanted to do and they said they would drive me to the border.

Once we got there, they walked with me to a Border Patrol agent. I gave her my paperwork and explained what happened. Naturally, she did not believe it, nor did her supervisors, so they held me while they verified everything. A couple days later I crossed the border at Brownsville, Texas into the United States of America."

Steve was filled with an incredible sense of curiosity. "What did it feel like when you walked into the United States?"

"I felt freedom," Fidel shouted. "It's hard to put into words what I felt, really, but I felt like a new dream had been born in me. I could work three jobs if I wanted to."

Steve thought that was hilarious. "Why would you want to do that?"

"Cuba is a Communist country, Steve, and you could only do one job, even if you wanted to do more. So coming here, I basically could do whatever I was willing to do. Eventually, I made my way to Miami where I did work three jobs. I worked at the airport. I sold cheesy t-shirts to tourists. And right before I left Miami, I was doing some janitorial work for a local real estate agent."

SHIFTING GEARS

"Why did I leave Miami?" Fidel said, asking the question before Steve had a chance to. "Because I wasn't learning the language or about American culture. If I stayed there, I might as well have stayed in Cuba. One night after cleaning up the real estate office, I turned on the computer at the front desk and searched the internet for the best places to live in the United States and up popped Colorado Springs. As far as I could tell, there were no Cubans there."

"That where you met the Janitor?"

"Purchased an old town car with the money I had saved. I wasn't thrilled to be driving again, but at least it was a little more upscale than a taxi," Fidel winked. "This was pre-Uber, so I would stake out hotels and conference centers between Denver and Colorado Springs to get customers."

"Gutsy."

"I had been driving people to and from this conference at The Broadmoor hotel conference all week. It was the same routine with every customer: jump in the back, confirm the destination, read a newspaper or whatever. No one ever engaged in conversation. I was dying to ask questions and figure out what these conferences they were attending were all about. The moment he got in the car, I knew something was different about him."

"How so?"

"The two things I remember about that drive. First, he asked for my name. No one had bothered to ask my name, ever! Isn't it unbelievable? The other was he sat in the front and started asking me questions, about my life and what my goals were. We talked the entire drive from Colorado Springs to Denver. When I dropped him off at the airport he offered to mentor me."

"Wow! What an incredible opportunity," Steve said. "I bet you were all over that."

"Actually, no," Fidel said self-consciously. "I said thank you and told him I would think about it. I really liked the sound of someone mentoring me, but I didn't believe he actually meant it."

Fidel took out his wallet and retrieved a faded, dog-eared business card. "Before getting out of the car, he handed me this card and invited me to call if I wanted to take him up on his offer. I never did."

"Wait, what?"

"I know, I know. It was one of my biggest regrets, too. There is no doubt that things would have been much easier had I been humble enough to accept his invitation."

"I'm confused. How did you guys end up working together?"

"During our drive, I shared that my big dream was to make millions in commercial real estate. He told me about the importance of investing in one's self and convinced me to purchase a study kit for the real estate license. I bought it that night, studied my butt off and passed the exam. My American dream was coming true, or so I thought."

"No one hired you," Steve guessed.

"Why do you think that is?"

"No one wanted to hire a kid with an accent, zero experience and no local market to draw from?

"Bingo. I didn't look like much on paper, but no one dug deeper to see how hard I was willing to work. Needless to say, getting going was a struggle for the first couple years."

Fidel leaned back in his chair. "Eventually someone took a chance on me. I outworked, outnegotiated everyone. About three years after driving The Janitor to the airport, I was in the middle of an intense negotiation on the purchase of a commercial property when the seller's agent said the owner wanted to come and participate in the negotiation. It was highly unusual and I was totally against it but I eventually gave in to pressure. The day comes along and I'm ready for battle and..."

"In walks The Janitor?"

"Yes!" Fidel said, throwing his hands up in disbelief. "He sat at the table and we started the negotiation. It was fierce but fair and we came to terms all parties could agree on. Then as we were walking out he pats me on the back and said, 'Fidel, you've come along way since dropping me off at the airport. I'm proud of you.'

Up until then, I didn't think he recognized me. I made sure not to miss the opportunity for his mentorship a second time. Before he left the building, I pitched to him the idea of me becoming his head of real estate to manage his personal and corporate holdings. He said I could start Monday and the rest is history."

The elevator doors dinged open. In walked the receptionist that had so kindly greeted Steve the day he met The Janitor. She was carrying a platter of PB & J sandwich wedges along with a few cups and a pitcher of milk.

"Thank you, Jessica," Fidel said placing the platter on the coffee table as Jessica returned to making clients and prospects feel welcome as they entered the building. "Have you had these before, Steve?"

"If those are what I think they are then, yes!"

Fidel proceeded to dip a sandwich wedge into a glass of milk. "The Janitor loves his PB & J, but his absence means more for us."

Fidel smiled while Steve devoured a couple wedges and washed them down with a glass of milk.

"How did you have the confidence to pitch The Janitor on your idea?" Steve asked taking another sip.

"I didn't. I knew I didn't really have all the skills and capabilities for the task, but I also knew that I could learn anything I didn't already know. So I went for it."

"And if he said no?"

"Well, at that point, the worst possible outcome would have been him saying thanks but no thanks. In that case, I would have been in the same spot I was in had I never asked."

"Good point."

"You know, you say you want to build confidence," Fidel said as he polished off a couple more wedges with a milk chaser. "Well, 'build' is the operative word and the tricky thing is that you're not going to wake up one day saying 'I'm confident.' Your thoughts determine your behavior, so you have to think confidently first. Then you have to start taking action every day with the understanding that you will fall down over and over again but also with the commitment that you will get back up.

I didn't just start running one day. I went from crawling to walking to running to falling to running a little bit differently to skipping to running faster to running for long distances and so on. And I'm still growing in confidence because the act of building is a lifelong pursuit. A learnable, repeatable skill—a process, not a destination."

Steve, clearly disappointed, slouched in his chair. "Making change is going to be hard."

"But staying put where you are, the way you are is not an option."

Fidel walked over to his desk, opened a drawer and retrieved a stack of white 3x5 cards which he proceeded to spread out all over the coffee table.

"I'm a visual learner, are you?"

"Sure."

"Right now, you're kind of like Shackleton and his men. They set sail with the objective to map Antarctica and even completed part of their original goal. But, as we know, their ship was crushed by the ice. Now, what was your objective?"

"It was always to have a positive impact on the lives of others, but I never had a clear vision or understanding of what it looked like or even could look like. Ultimately, it became about me gaining status and accolades and making money."

"Nothing wrong with being ambitious as long as it aligns with your customers' needs. In fact, I would be more concerned if you had no ambition. Okay, now your ship, let's call it..."

"Outlier."

"Okay, the ship called Outlier brought you this far in your journey, but it has also been crushed by elements mostly beyond your control."

Steve was listening attentively as Fidel moved all of the cards to the center of the coffee table to form a large pile.

"Now. You are here," Fidel continued, placing his finger in the center of the pile. "Smack-dab in the middle of this iceberg that the waves, currents, winds, swells and tides have smashed together with other icebergs to form one big frozen island. Got it?"

"Yes."

"Great. Now I want you to close your eyes and visualize it. I want you to go there in your mind."

"Um, what? How do I..."

"Just close your eyes. Take a few deep breaths and imagine you're sitting in the middle of this iceberg with Shackleton and his men. Let me know when you can see it."

Steve closed his eyes and leaned back in his chair.

"Okay."

"Day in and day out, you're sitting on the ice. Weeks and months go by. The cold, the wind, the seal meat, wet clothes, wet blankets and salty water. All of it has become your new normal. And you, like the men of *Endurance*, started to acclimate to this new normal and begin to grow comfortable. You even start to feel a certain sense of security. It's happening to you, right now."

"I don't want that to happen to me," Steve said with a shiver.

"Are you willing to die on that block of ice?"

"No!"

"Then you have to do exactly what Shackleton and his men did."

"And what was that?"

"Remind themselves of the seriousness of their situation. Acknowledge the fact that shifting tides will always be there. Recognize that the only way to avoid getting crushed is to prepare to get off the iceberg before it breaks into an unknowable number of pieces. But that awareness doesn't come without knowing what's at stake. This was true for them, it is true for me and it's true for you. It's those decisions—big and small—followed by action that will determine our legacy just as much as it did for Shackleton and his crew."

"Okay, so how do I proceed?"

Fidel paused for a moment before answering. "I believe there are some better questions that every great leader should stop and consider first."

Steve felt his face blush with excitement that Fidel implied he was a great leader.

"What's at stake? Like I said before, I believe that is the first question you should reflect on. Why does it matter? That's another question that will build upon your answers to the first. The last question: when does this become real? I'll give you a hint on how to tackle that one. If you wait until the ice breaks for it to become real, then you're too late. If you invest in reflecting on these three questions the answer to the 'how' question will nearly always become clear."

"I appreciate you sharing so openly with me," Steve said reaching out across the coffee table to shake Fidel's hand. "Thank you."

Fidel stood up and confidently placed both his hands on Steve's.

"This is the beginning of something special, Steve, and I am glad to be on the journey with you. Let's connect again in a couple weeks and see how those questions are treating you. Sound good?"

"Very generous. Consider it done. See you tomorrow?"

"Yes, sir. Dinner at The Janitor's is always something special. Plus, I wouldn't want to miss seeing the surprise he has for you," Fidel concluded with a toothy smile.

REFLECT AND RESPOND

THOUGHTS FROM STEVE'S JOURNAL

My story. My gifts. Has a lack of clarity and ownership prevented me from seeing and taking the action that I've known I need to take? Have I been sitting on an island waiting for something or someone to take action for me? Apple, Google, Buzz Aldrin, Shackleton and his crew: what do they all have in common? They had big visions, yes, but that is not it. They realized the importance of the moment and they had the courage to take the next step to accomplish their objectives with urgency and with intention. They may not have been in possession of the exact answer. but they were willing to think about and explore what was at stake, why it all mattered and they allowed it to be real in the here and now. This is not to say that failure didn't happen or hurt their ego, but they allowed certain dreams to die so the real adventure could begin. They controlled their narrative. They didn't care about status as much as they cared about creating something that people would remember. I want that! This is not to say they were perfect. There is no perfect, unblemished example. Like the best athletes, I have to visualize taking action and see myself in control, but I also needed to see how I respond when my ship is scuttled. Will I allow myself to remain stranded or will I recognize where I am and do everything in my power to get off the iceberg? We live in the most abundant time in the history of mankind. If Shackleton and his men can sail down to Antarctica and survive for nearly two years on nothing but blubber and melted ice for water—well, what more am I capable of? I will not buy into the myth that there isn't any opportunity out there. I have to get off the iceberg and go get it. I will take responsibility for my action.

REFLECT

- Why is having a false sense of security dangerous?

- How would taking action provide you a sense of freedom? Why is it important?

- How have some of my dreams been crushed? Why do I hold onto them?

- What is at stake for me? Why does it matter?

- When will it become real for me?

- When have I felt momentum in the past?
  What was I doing?

RESPOND

- What is one thing I am willing to do today?
  Why?

- How will I map the next best steps after
  that?

- How will I build up and maintain momentum?

- How will releasing old dreams free me to
  realize new ones?

- How will I approach setting goals and identifying
  milestones? What tools will I use?

Part 5
COMMUNITY

LUCY MEETS THE JANITOR

"You almost ready, honey?" Steve asked sliding his arms into his sports coat in front of the bedroom mirror. "I don't want to be late."

Lucy took a few steps out of their walk-in closet and spun around. Steve caught her reflection in the mirror and, for a moment, time moved in slow motion. She looked so happy and so beautiful. It was exactly as he remembered her before all hell broke loose in their life. And without even thinking, Steve quietly expressed gratitude for the opportunity their challenges provided them to rejuvenate their marriage.

Steve turned and pulled her into his chest.

"You know, sometimes it's hard to see."

"Hard to see what?" Lucy asked, cocking her head back so she could look at in his eyes.

"To see just how good I've got it." Steve pressed her in even closer to him. "I'm sorry it took nearly dying for my eyes to open."

Lucy smiled and rested her head in the bend of Steve's neck.

"We both lost sight. I'm in the boat with you. We get another chance to do it right!"

Lucy pushed back from Steve and spun around once more.

"So," Lucy said with a sassy smile. "How do I look?"

"Radiant!"

"You don't think I'm overdressed?"

"You're perfect."

Just then Tina and Elle came running up to Steve with the babysitter chasing not far behind. They tackled his legs, causing him to topple over on top of them, laughing.

Lucy knelt down and scooped the wily girls up in her arms.

"You girls be on your best behavior tonight, okay?"

"Where are you going, Mommy?" Tina asked.

"To Daddy's friend's house for dinner."

"You look like a princess," Elle said with a giggle.

Steve stood up, straightened his coat and then lifted the girls off of the ground, twirling them around saying, "Does that make me a prince?"

Both the girls were giggling wildly.

"No, silly," both exclaimed.

Steve put the girls down and grabbed the keys from his dresser.

"We'll give you a hug, kiss and blessing when we get home. In the meantime, may I escort the princess?" Steve asked inviting Lucy to place her arm in his. "Her chariot awaits."

"You may," Lucy said with an exaggerated curtsy.

As they pulled away from the driveway, Lucy sighed as she reached across and placed her hand in Steve's.

"Who's sighing now. Nervous?"

"A little. More curious than nervous." Lucy pivoted in her seat and looked at Steve. "What if they don't like me?"

"Not like you!" Steve laughed. "Not possible! But if you decide you want to leave, excuse yourself to call the babysitter and that will be my cue that it's time to go."

"No, I'll be fine. Just don't leave me."

"Never."

There were several other cars in The Janitor's driveway when Steve pulled in. He looked at Lucy and gave her a knowing smile as he squeezed her hand. "Sorry we're late."

"It's okay. At least we are fashionably late," Steve winked.

Steve parked the car and got out to open the door for Lucy. "You weren't kidding," Lucy said as she looked around the front of the property. "This place is stunning. I feel like I stepped into the cover of one of those high-end real estate magazines."

"Wait until you see inside."

Lucy hooked her arm with Steve's and they walked to the front door.

"Ready?" Steve said looking at Lucy.

"Ready."

Steve rang the doorbell, and a few moments later The Janitor swung open the door.

"Welcome to my home," The Janitor exclaimed as he ushered them in. "So honored you could make it."

"This is my wife, Lucy. And Lucy this is the..." Steve paused and laughed to himself. "You know, I'm sorry.

This whole time I've never stopped to ask your real name."

The Janitor smiled.

"That's perfectly alright. Most people call me The Janitor, but my real name is Nathaniel."

Nathaniel, Steve thought to himself. *He looks like a Nathaniel.*

"Well then," Steve continued. "Lucy, this is Nathaniel."

Nathaniel put his arm out to escort Lucy into the rest of the house.

"So Lucy, do you like peanut butter and jelly sandwiches?"

Lucy looked back at Steve and mouthed OMG.

"Only if they come with a cold glass of milk."

"We're in for a great evening," Nathaniel said, "Let's join everyone down in the cellar."

Steve lingered in the entry with his hands in his pockets, marveling at all that had transpired.

"If you stay there all night, you'll miss out on the surprise that I told you about."

"Surprise? What surprise?"

Nathaniel turned and whispered in Lucy's ear and then looked back at Steve with a smile. "Now let's go enjoy some of Angelica's PB & Js."

Meeting Bill

Gerald was waiting at the bottom of the steps for Steve. At first, he felt a flash of anger as he made his way down the spiral staircase, but it disappeared as quickly as it came and a deep sense of gratitude took its place.

"Hello, Steve," Gerald said reaching out to shake Steve's hand. "Nathaniel invited me to join you all for dinner. I hope you don't mind."

Steve hesitated for a moment and then grabbed Gerald's hand and pulled him into a bear hug. "I am glad you are able to join us. If it weren't for you firing me and then connecting me with The Jan—I mean, Nathaniel, I wouldn't be here either."

"Let's face it," Gerald said looking at Nathaniel. "If it weren't for him, I don't think any of us would be in this room right now. We're all in for a treat tonight."

Steve nodded in agreement. As he scanned the room, he reflected on the fact that just a few days earlier, he was exploring his own story and journey in this cellar, surrounded by these bottles of wine, each one with its own unique and imperfect manuscript. Now, the most important person in his life was in the same room, surrounded by the same bottles, dipping PB & Js into cold milk with Nathaniel, Chaz, Fidel, Gerald and Bill, who Steve was yet to meet.

With a lightweight gingham shirt and a busy bow tie, Bill was the epitome of a well-dressed Southern gentleman. His age wasn't clear, but with his smartly-combed, silver hair he had to be at least the same age as The Janitor.

Nathaniel looked at Steve with a smile and then tapped his glass full of milk with a spoon from the table that had been set for dinner. "Before we sit down for dinner, I would like to propose a toast."

A server appeared from behind the wine racks with an unopened bottle of champagne and little spoon-fuls of appetizer.

"You didn't think PB & Js and cold milk were the only menu items tonight, did you?" Nathaniel said with a laugh. "In those tiny spoons is some sort of magic the chef upstairs created to prepare our palates for the amazing meal that we are about to ex-perience."

Steve and the others proceeded to consume the spoonfuls of goodness while the server popped open the bubbly and proceeded to fill everyone's glasses.

Clearing his throat, Nathaniel continued. "We all get misled by the destination from time to time when we know the joy is really in the walking, or in Fidel's case, the running. Well, recently our new friend, Steve, embarked on quite the journey. You've no doubt learned some invaluable lessons over the past few days and, if you choose, the insights they provide will continue to manifest throughout your life," Nathaniel continued, raising his glass toward Steve.

"So here's to Steve! We are all honored to be on this path with you."

With glasses raised, they all responded in unison. "To Steve!"

Steve could feel the blood rush to his face as he began to blush. Lucy, who was wiping a tear away, came to his side and took his arm into hers.

As Nathaniel turned his attention back to the rest of his guests, he continued, "But community is where all of this comes together and thrives. We are wired to be, and feel, connected. The more fun we have together, the better each of us will be and do, individually and collectively. So tonight, let's have fun while we learn. And with that in mind, I want to introduce you to my dear friend, Bill. He is not just a friend, but a mentor and coach to me. He's guided me to some personal insights, and I hope he can do the same for you. Bill, the floor is yours."

Bill remained standing as the rest of Nathaniel's guests sat at the table.

"It's an honor to be among you tonight, but I have some disappointing news for you all—I'm not here to teach. I'm here to help facilitate a conversation. Is that okay?"

"Take it away," Gerald hollered.

"Great!" Bill said handing out blank pieces of paper and pens. "These are for you to take notes or write down any questions or thoughts to contribute as we share ideas this evening. As you might be able to tell from my accent, I grew up in the South. Louisiana to be precise. My dad was not in the picture growing up, so my brother and I ended up spending a lot of time with my grandfather, who we called, PawPaw. He was a man's man and one of the most influential people in my life.

He taught me many lessons as a kid. Some involved a belt and my rear end, but most took place between these four walls," Bill said, pointing to his head. The most important lesson he shared with me took place one summer night when I was about eight years old. He dropped us off at my mother's house after a week of camping in the wilderness. It was late, maybe 10 p.m., and as he was helping to get us settled in our beds, my younger brother cried out, 'Spider!' Sure enough, PawPaw went over to my brother's bed to took care of the arachnid. But another spider, and then another appeared before he even left my brother's bedside."

Lucy cringed. "Disgusting. A spider nest?"

"Exactly."

"I can't stand spiders," Chaz remarked.

"Me neither," Steve said. "They creep me out."

"PawPaw got us both up out of our beds and stood us in the doorway while he lifted up our mattresses and started to clean. There was so much clutter in, on, around and under our bed. He just quietly went to work and didn't mutter a single word. By the time he was done," Bill continued, "he had vacuumed our entire room and organized our toys, dirty clothes, bags...everything was where it should be."

"Wow, he was generous," Fidel laughed. "My mom would have grabbed me by the ear and held on until my room was immaculate."

The room erupted in laughter.

"Before he left, he sat us both on our beds and said, 'Boys your environment matters but the things you allow in your environment matters even more. You created an environment for those buggers to move in, make a nest and spin their webs. I cleaned things up this once because we all make mistakes, but settling for them is not acceptable. If you don't want to get bit by spiders, then don't make space for them to move in. Do you understand?' All we did was nod and then went straight to sleep. It may have been the best night's sleep I've ever had, knowing that I wasn't going to get bit by any spiders."

"Can you send him over to our house?" Steve said. "I think my girls could use the same lesson."

Lucy elbowed Steve in the ribs.

"Hey, I'm just joking."

"The lesson my PawPaw taught me that night has carried over into the rest of my life including my friendships, business deals and other things I say yes to. I'd like you to write down these questions:

In what environment do you spend the most time?
Who is with you?
What is being said?

Then when you are ready, I'd like for us to share our answers with each other."

While the group was writing down their thoughts, Nathaniel waved to one of the servers, whispered something to him and then turned his attention to his own piece of paper.

"How are we doing?" Bill asked taking a sip of his champagne. "Need another minute?"

Chaz raised her hand. "At first I wrote down my studio, but then I thought for another moment and realized the environment I spend the most time in is my head."

Bill smiled and nodded his head.

"Did anyone else write that down?" Bill asked.

One by one Steve, Lucy, Fidel, Gerald and Nathaniel raised their hands. And just as they did that the two servers came and delivered the first course along with fresh glasses of wine.

"Now isn't that interesting. And who is with you?"

"I'll speak from my personal experience," Fidel began, looking around the table. "It's the naysayers. They are the ones in my head. The people that told me I couldn't make it, that said I should know my place, that I should have stayed in Cuba and been a cab driver, that said stop acting like I've been there before."

Fidel picked up his fork and started to shuffle the food around on his plate.

Nathaniel noticed no one had started to eat. "It's okay everyone, we can talk with our mouth's full tonight."

"Just don't tell the kids," Lucy winked at Steve.

Fidel took a bite and continued his story. "After the Mexican authorities released us, I met this couple and they gave me a Bible. My family wasn't religious, so I had never owned or read one. While we were driving to the border, they told me the story about David and Goliath. And I became fixated on a particular moment. The battle is raging on and David, a young shepherd boy at the time, shows up expecting to see the fight. Instead, he finds the Israelite army cowering in the trenches.

"He walks up to his brothers and said, 'Why is no one fighting?' To which his brothers—the naysayers—responded, 'Go back to your sheep. You're just a shepherd boy. You don't belong here.' And David looked at them and said, 'Watch me.' And the rest is history. Sometimes I feel I can respond like David, but other times I succumb to the pressure of the naysayers. But that is just me."

Steve was surprised by Chaz and Fidel's answers. Here he was, surrounded by these people who had accomplished such great things, who had provided him with so much insight, and they struggled inside their head just like him.

"It's not just you," Lucy started. "I had all the potential in the world to be a top marketing executive. When push came to shove, I decided that what I really wanted was to be the chief executive officer at home. My parents, whom I love and adore, just couldn't understand it. They told me I was wasting my talents and gifts, but in my core, I knew my talents could be delivered anywhere and that my children would benefit from them most. It's not always easy, but it was definitely the right call."

Bill raised his glass. "Thank you for sharing. We have to realize that socialization by definition wants everyone to be average. And so when someone is trying to stand apart, others are not going to like it. They are going to challenge you and say things like you're going to fail. If we aren't aware of this, what happens is we start thinking this way in our own heads and that affects our willingness to take action."

"Ain't that the truth," Gerald said raising his glass and taking a sip of wine. "I don't think I've ever shared this with you, Bill, but when Nathaniel put us in touch so many years ago I thought all of this stuff was just psychobabble. But when I took your advice and began to surround myself with people who would encourage me to have big ideas and take risks, who would help keep my confidence at a high level, but also hold me accountable when they saw me making mistakes, boy, did things change. It's why I stay so close to guys like Nathaniel, and hopefully my new and old friends here at this table."

THE STUFF

Steve was vigorously taking notes as people were talking and sharing their thoughts. "I have a few things I'd like to add to that," Steve chimed in timidly.

"Please do," Bill said.

Steve looked at his notes and started to read. "Okay, the first thing is that pursuing great things can be lonely. The second thing is I used to believe that once I got in a groove it would be smooth sailing, but it's not. Since meeting all of you, I've learned this stuff is hard; it requires a lot of regular work and a little bit of friction isn't a bad thing."

Steve paused while the servers cleared the plates to make room for the next course.

"The last one is kind of tied to the first. Having people in your life to help normalize things during rough patches will make you feel less alone, make the hard work more tolerable and prevent those creepy spiders from building a nest in your head," Steve concluded with a cheeky grin.

"Bravo, Steve, bravo," Nathaniel clapped. "That's good stuff!"

"I shared this with Fidel," Steve continued, "but I'm kind of stuck with the question: does this stuff work in the real world? I want it to believe it, but I don't know. I'm struggling."

"I think the answers to your question are sitting at this table," Bill said empathetically. "Will it be easy? Absolutely not. Will it be challenging? You bet. Will it take time? Yes. How much? It depends. Can you face it alone? No. Don't get me wrong, you guys. It's true that success loves speed. But too many of us forsake the richness of the human experience for efficiency and we short ourselves in the process. Let me ask you a question, Steve, do you want to go fast, or would you rather go far?"

"Far, for sure. Fast is fun initially but burning out is not."

"I would agree with you, Steve. How about you guys?" Bill asked, looking around at the rest of the table. Each one responding the same, "Far."

Bill picked up his glass and swirled the wine around before taking a sip. "When it comes to community, what do you think I really mean?"

Lucy raised her hand. "Friendship?"

"Exactly. It is the stuff of community! And it's more than simply passing time with someone you enjoy. I like to hang out and relax just as much as the next guy, but in the pursuit to unlock and fulfill our potential, friendship requires us to go deeper. What do you think, Steve?"

"What would I be looking for in that type of friendship?"

"Think about it like layers," Nathaniel jumped in. "Each layer that you peel off leads you closer to the core. In my experience, the first layer of a deep friendship is wild curiosity."

"Wild curiosity! Love that," Bill said writing it down on his own sheet of paper. "Please elaborate."

"Well, to me, it means that the friend cares about your success as much as, if not more than, his own. And it's wild because it doesn't make sense to people on the outside looking in."

"Then you're a phenomenal friend," Fidel interrupted. "You have always been wildly curious about my success. And I think the others would probably say the same."

"Amen to that!" Gerald hollered. "That type of friendship has made room for me to share my deepest desires and fears."

As the servers delivered the main course, Steve looked around the table and thought to himself, *Everyone has been wildly curious about me, but I'm not sure if I have been curious enough about them.*

"Mmmm. Pomme frites and steak!" Chaz interrupted as she picked up the plate the servers just placed in front of her. "Definitely one of my favorites."

"How do you know if you're being curious enough?" Lucy asked while she waited for her plate to be served.

Steve was grateful that someone else asked the question.

"I was just about to ask the same question, but then it hit me," Chaz began while cutting into a juicy piece of steak. "Collaboration. When I find myself alone with all my mental spiders, it's because I'm not being curious. And I'm not being curious because I'm not collaborating."

Lucy nodded in agreement as she made a note. "So instead of collaborating, your energy is wasted on making sure others are seeing things from your point of view?"

"I think about it this way. As an artist, I must recognize that I don't play for myself or for my own pleasure alone. How boring would that be! I mean practice alone, maybe. But perform alone. No thanks! Even if you're part of an ensemble—the camaraderie may be great but what good is all of it if no one hears you? After all, the ensemble already knows they sound amazing," Chaz said with a wink.

Chaz's energy and passion about the topic had captivated the room. Even the servers were standing the back, hanging on her every word.

"So, in your example, collaboration is something bigger than simply working with other musicians or experts in your field?" Lucy asked.

"Bigger, way bigger!" Chaz continued as she sliced once again into the juicy steak. "The audience. In my shows, there might be a dozen musicians but there are hundreds..."

"Hey, don't short yourself, Chaz!" Nathaniel interrupted. "You've performed in Madison Square Garden with thousands of fans."

Chaz blushed.

"You're right. I did. Thank you. But the point is—regardless of the size of the audience—if you collaborate with them and find a way to make them a part of the performance, they can really bring whatever you're playing to life. The intention, the heart, the soul and the passion all create a synergy between the performer and the audience. It's an ebb and flow of giving and receiving. Doesn't mean you can't enjoy performing a solo from time to time; just that without community, without someone to play with or for, it's a little pointless."

"You're on fire, Chaz!" Fidel clapped.

Chaz stood up and gave an exaggerated bow. "I try, I try," she said, laughing.

"What happens if you get off track? If your solo has gone on a little too long or maybe missed it all together?" Steve asked.

"The next layer would be accountability, don't you think?" Bill asked the group as he stabbed some of the pomme frites on his plate.

"Is there another word for accountability? Something with a 'C'?" Fidel asked. "We've got a theme going with curiosity and collaboration."

"Good idea. How about correction?"

"Can we skip that layer altogether?" Lucy asked half seriously. "Both words make me feel uncomfortable."

"Why is that?"

Lucy shifted in her seat. "I don't think many of us enjoy being told what to do."

"What if correction was less about telling people what to do and more about reminding them of who they are, why they are pursuing what they are pursuing and who they are capable of becoming? Would it be more acceptable in that context?"

"I suppose that's where the rubber meets the road," Steve agreed. "But the ability to correct someone is earned, right?"

"Yes! If you don't spend time being curious and collaborating, you'll never really know what the individual needs to be reminded of when they veer off track. If you didn't earn the right, then correcting them comes off as..." Bill said pointing to Lucy.

"Telling them what to do."

"Which, as Lucy indicated earlier, no one likes."

Fidel picked up his fork and tapped the side of his glass to get everyone's attention. "Bill, you mentioned that developing these habits and these friendships will take time and I have been fighting with that idea in my head. It just dawned on me, and I believe it's important to note, that the length of time spent in any of these layers is less important than the actual acts of being curious, collaborating and, when necessary, correcting incongruent thinking."

"How so," asked Gerald.

"Just look at Nathaniel," Fidel continued lightheartedly. "He's great at correcting and reminding."

"It's only because Bill was a good teacher."

"As everyone knows, I first met him driving to the airport. I was curious about him, but he was wildly curious about me. We only spent ninety minutes together, then I didn't see him for a very long time. In fact the next time I saw him was across the negotiating table, but during that drive to the airport, he helped set me on a path that ultimately put me in a position to work alongside him. And while I was his employee, whenever I would get off track, or try to fly solo for too long or encounter mental spiders, as Bill put it, he would stop me and correct me by asking me three questions:

What are you doing here?
Why not you?
Why not now?

He never provided the answers, but instead used the opportunity to correct me as a reminder."

"Funny," Steve smiled, looking at Nathaniel, "he's asked me some very similar questions."

"With that," Fidel said raising his glass. "I invite you all to join me in toasting the man we affectionately call The Janitor. Here's to many more years of wild curiosity, collaboration and, yes, even correction."

"Here, here," the table declared in a chorus as everyone clicked their glasses together.

"We've covered a lot this evening," Nathaniel continued, "so let's spend the rest of our time together enjoying our food and practicing some of these concepts and questions. What do you say, Bill?"

"Excellent idea. Let's see. Gerald and Steve, you guys pair up. Then Chaz and Lucy. And Fidel and Nathaniel. For now, let's focus on developing that sense of wild curiosity. Each person take 10 minutes and just ask questions of each other: hopes, dreams, fears, aspirations, successes, failures, Angelica's secret PB & J recipe," Bill winked. "I will walk around and help facilitate the conversation or answer any questions that may pop up. And by the time we're done dessert should be here."

Nathaniel got up and walked over to Steve. "Don't you worry," Nathaniel whispered in Steve's ear. "Your surprise is still coming. Should be here around the same time as dessert."

"I completely forgot! Something's being delivered?" Steve asked. "I know it's too late, but you didn't have to."

"I know, I know. Now go be wildly curious with Gerald. What a great opportunity for a fresh start!"

THE SURPRISE

This new community of friends was fully engaged in wild curiosity when the chef and the team of servers came walking down the staircase holding trays of freshly baked goods. The sweet aroma quickly filled the room while Bill brought everyone back together.

"Dessert's here, which means time is up."

"Wow," Nathaniel said walking over to the chef. "Look at that. Doesn't everything look delicious? Do I have to share?"

"It's up to you," the chef laughed.

"Let's give the chef and his team a hand for all of the wonderful food that they created and the experience they helped to curate."

Applause filled the cellar with sounds of gratitude and thanksgiving.

"There is one other thing," the chef began to say. "I've been told there is a special surprise at the door for one of your guests."

Steve suddenly felt very warm and started to blush.

"That would be for you, Steve," Nathaniel said with a grin.

Lucy placed her hand on Steve's back and gently pushed him forward.

"Go," Lucy whispered.

"Go?"

"Upstairs. For your surprise."

Steve turned and looked at his beloved bride. "Well, aren't you coming with me?"

Lucy tilted her head, her eyes welling with tears. "No, my love," Lucy said smiling lovingly at her husband. "Nathaniel told me about the surprise when we were walking to the cellar. I think it would be better for you to go up alone. Besides, Chaz and I were just about to exchange makeup tips. You can share the surprise with us when you come back down."

"You're sure?"

"I'm sure."

"Why are you crying then?"

"Just excited for you is all."

"Excited? What kind of surprise is this?" Steve pulled Lucy close. "I'm glad we are here together."

Steve turned back toward Nathaniel, the chef, the servers and the tray of delights that they were holding. "Let me guess. You're all staying down here, too."

"You guessed correctly," Nathaniel winked at him as he picked a cookie up from the tray.

Steve wound his way up the staircase, through the kitchen and to the entryway where the surprise was waiting. When he arrived, he paused in shock. Standing there in the entryway was his father with his arms crossed behind his back.

"Dad! What are you doing here? How did you get here? Is everything okay?"

His dad smiled and looked back at Steve. "Yes, son. Everything is fine. Somehow, and I still haven't figured it out, Nathaniel managed to get a hold of my number and invited me to..."

"He called you?"

"Yeah. One minute I'm watching reruns of *The Price is Right* and the next minute I'm arranging travel plans to fly out to surprise you."

"You're the surprise?"

"Well, is it a nice surprise?" Steve's dad asked sheepishly.

"Yes. Sorry. Just a bit stunned. I didn't know what to expect, actually, but I never imagined the surprise would be you. What did he say to you?"

"He said he was a friend of yours, that he had heard about an unfinished game of catch and wondered if I'd be interested in finishing it. I told him I'd been dreaming of the day."

Steve began to get emotional.

"So?"

"So, what?"

"What do you say?" Steve's dad said tossing him a football. "Shall we go out front and pick up where we left off?"

Steve rushed to his father and wrapped him in his arms.

"It would mean the world to me."

Steve stopped at the door as he was following his dad outside. Not because he was having second thoughts or was angry, fearful or anxious. It was quite the opposite.

"You coming, son?"

He was aware there would always be work to do. But now that he had taken hold of the keys needed to unlock his potential, he was confident he'd be up for the task.

"Toss me the ball, old man," Steve shouted to his dad.

And as he ran outside, catching the ball, he knew the best was now and the best was still yet to come.

REFLECT AND RESPOND

THOUGHTS FROM STEVE'S JOURNAL

Community connects everything together. Friends, true friends are wildly curious about my desires just as much as they are of their own. So much so that they want to find ways to collaborate and help me realize them. Because I too am a good friend, I am equally as curious and eager to collaborate with and support them. A community of friends like this takes time to understand my story, my gifts and encourage me to take action. Most importantly, when something is amiss they hold me accountable, or as we decided—correct me. But this is something that is earned. When I am thinking poorly about something, they have the permission to correct me. When I am doing something that is not like myself, they have permission to challenge and if necessary correct me. It may be painful at times but this comes from a place of love. I had no idea what I was missing. Doing things alone seemed easier to me because I didn't have to be accountable to or vulnerable with anyone. Nope, it was just me alone with my thoughts. But the byproduct of being part of a community that is curious about you, wants to collaborate with you and even challenge or correct you is the realization that everyone is just like me. We all want to do things that matter. We all are afraid of the pain of regret. We all are afraid of being alone. Realizing this means that

I can be braver in the areas that matter most. The bond of community will be forged by facing challenges together. Community makes victories sweeter and dulls the sting of defeat.

REFLECTION

- Where do I find community now? Why have I sought community there?

- Who can I make room for and bring into my pursuits?

- Who has been wildly curious about my success?

- Who have I enjoyed collaborating with? Why?

- Who will fight for me and my hopes and dreams?

- Who will challenge and correct me when I'm not living up to my potential?

- How has community/friendship affected the relationship I have with my story, gifts and ability to act?

RESPOND

- How can I surprise someone with my support and encouragement?

- How can I continue to build connection with those who have shown me support?

- How can I invite others to challenge or correct me when I am not living up to my potential?

- Who will my Future Five be in each of the original six caves: Faith, Family, Friends, Fitness, Finances and Fun?

- Why have I chosen them?

- How will I reach out to them?

- How will I approach setting goals and identifying milestones? What tools will I use?

Giving Thanks

How do I begin to thank the myriad lives who have helped to mold me into the man I am becoming? I suppose, the most appropriate place to begin with is the one who has given me life—God. I am grateful to God for the life he has given to me. For the ups, downs, wins, losses, hardships, joys...for all of it. It may have taken me a while, but I have finally realized that all of it has been to prepare me for the journey that is to come.

One of the greatest gifts God has blessed me with is my family. We are just as dysfunctional as the next family. And still, despite all of our shortcomings we love each other—fiercely. This love has been demonstrated to my siblings and me through the witness of my parents, Michael and Pamela. I will always be grateful for the many sacrifices that you made along the way so that we might be able to enjoy a life better than what you experienced. Dad, you are a quiet warrior. You are slow to anger and rich in kindness. We haven't always had the best relationship, but I will always be grateful for the example of duty, loyalty and sacrifice that you shared with me. Mom, your belief in me and my God-given abilities has been unceasing. Even when I have doubted, you have fought to remind me of the man I am capable of becoming. To my siblings—Joy, John, Mary, Katie and Joe—you have been some of my greatest champions. We each possess so many wonderful gifts. I can't wait to see they impact they have in the world.

As The Janitor teaches Steve, friendships are truly the greatest treasure. And in that case, I am a very rich man.

Zach and Alexis, you are my oldest friends and have always been in my corner. You have helped carry me through some of the most challenging periods of my life and been alongside me to make my victories sweeter. Your faithfulness and love will never be forgotten.

Brendan and Colleen, the two of you are front and center in some of the most monumental (and embarrassing) moments of my life over the last 15 years. Life would be much less colorful without you and your family in it. Oh..and don't forget the wine.

Matt, Brooke, Mad, Joel, Olivia and Zeke: I am incredibly grateful for your love, support and for breathing life into my dreams and listening to my wild ideas.

Rob and Valjean, you are my second set of parents. Thank you for breathing life into me.

To my dear friends from my mastermind: Joanna, Meghann, Dave, Jesse and Nick. Thank you for adding to my heart.

To friends who specifically offered to read and test some of the ideas of the book along the way. Specifically, Dan, Meghann, Chris, Ryan, Nick and the others who I am probably forgetting.

To Greg Amundson and the CrossFit Amundson family, especially the 4 p.m. warriors, thank you. We are stronger together.

There are so many others who I could thank–you know who you are–but I am afraid I might miss someone so I am gathering you all together in this statement: THANK YOU!

Much of the content and ideas from this book are the fruit of conversations had with my guests on The Impact Entrepreneur Show. Before I thank the guests, I would like to honor Kelly and her team at the Lawton Marketing Group, as well as Cody, Ben, Zach, Hayden and the rest of the team at Podcast Masters. The podcast would not happen without them.

I want thank my guests. As of writing this, I have recorded nearly two hundred conversations with some incredible people. In order of appearance: Nancy Hawley, Sarak Kalick, Jordan Harbinger, Amy Cosper, Daniel Harkavy, Dave Kerpen, Cameron Herold, Anthony Iannarino, Susie Miller, Jon Vroman, Kelsey Humphreys, Dan Waldschmidt, Ian Utile, Aaron Hinde, Kelly Roach, Brian Dickinson, Tom Bilyeu, Honoree Corder, Bob Burg, Geoff Woods, Chris Faddis, Jason and Jodi Womack, Ryan Michler, Ryan Hawk, Kelly Starrett, Jocko Willink, AmyK Hutchens, Aaron Walker, Bernie Swain, David Dennis, Matthew Swinnerton, Justis Earle, Greg Amundson, AJ Hawk, Juliet Starrett, Tyler Fox, Rachel Balkovec, Erin Cafaro MacKenzie, Jim Afremow, Nicholas Kusmich, Mike Dillard, Michael Sacca, Evan Carmichael, Justin

Constantine, Noah Galloway, Steven Kotler, Stephan Aarstol, Don Wettrick, Ryan Evans, Sheryl O'Loughlin, JP Sears, Doug Kisgen, Jason Kotecki, Nick DiNardo, Cindi Busenhart, Adam Eidson, Lou Holtz, Todd Stottlemyre, Ken Kannappan, Steve Sims, Brad Stulberg, Dr. John Berardi, Marie Forleo, Colby Jubenville, Kevin Hall, Mel Robbins, Julie Scher, Josh Mantz, Jason Redman, Carey Lohrenz, Rebecca Jackson, Blake Jamieson, Lauren Mayhew, Kelly Clements, Dr. Issac Jones, Kara Goldin, Eren Bali, Kevin Lacz, Jon Gordon, Daniel McGinn, Lisa Flynn, Steve Olsher, Dana Cavalea, Christmas Abbott, Chris Sajnog, Caroline Burckle, Rebecca Soni, Andy Janning, Patrick Lencioni, Nathan Ogden, Bo Burlingham, Craig Ballantyne, John Caglione, Jr., Derek Clark, Malorie Tadimi, Zach Obront, Jesse Itzler, Armando Cruz, Jason Coombs, Dorcas Cheng-Tozun, Nick Craig, Rusty Labuschagne, Bill Hart, Dave Evans, Cara Miller, Christopher Lochhead, Rick Miller, Carrie Rose, Jeff Moreno, Flynn Cochran, Jessica Turner, Tony Grebmeier, Larry Hagner, Jessica Honegger, Eli Bremer, Chris Voss, Ike Ndolo, Nic McKinley, John O'Leary, Marc Gutman, Dr. Nick Hyde and the many other guests to come.

Finally, thank you for reading and listening. I believe in you and can't wait to see the impact mastering your key has in the world.

God bless!

ABOUT MIKE

Mike Flynn has been advising individuals, as well as executives of companies large and small since 2005. And beginning in 2009, he felt called to do something more, something even greater. Mike commenced that journey in 2015 when he launched a podcast called The Impact Entrepreneur Show. Since then, he has had nearly 200 one-on-one conversations with some of the world's most elite athletes, thinkers and entrepreneurs in an effort to discover how they are using their personal stories to have a game changing impact in the lives of others.

He makes his debut as an author with the release of a powerful story called Master The Key: A Story To Free Your Potential, Find Mean and Live Life On Purpose. The great Lou Holtz referred to it as a "must read," Mel Robbins called it an "inspiring story," and others have said it is a "fictional story that leads readers to the truth." In addition to writing for Huffington Post and Thrive Global, Mike has also given keynote speeches for regional offices of major corporations, such as New York Life and Keller Williams. If you would like to connect with Mike, please reach out via Instagram @theimpactmike or via his website www. theimpactentrepreneur.net